Winter Skills

Also by Rob Hunter

The Outdoor Companion (Constable, 1979)

By Rob Hunter, published by Spurbooks

Ski Touring, 1979
Walking
Map and Compass (with Terry Brown), 3rd Ed. 1981
Camping and Backpacking Cookbook, 1979
Jogging, 1979
Cross Country Skiing, 1977
Outdoor First Aid (with Terry Brown), 2nd Ed. 1980
Weather Lore (with Terry Brown), 2nd Ed. 1980
Sailing (with Terry Brown), 2nd Ed. 1981
Chart and Compass, 1978
Snorkelling (with Terry Brown), 2nd Ed. 1981
Survival and Rescue (with Terry Brown), 2nd Ed. 1980
Winter Camping (with Terry Brown), 1977
Knots, Bends and Hitches (with Terry Brown), 4th Ed. 1981
Parallel Skiing, 1977

Travel Guides by Rob Hunter (as Neil Lands)

The Dordogne, 1975
Beyond the Dordogne, 1977
Languedoc—Roussillon, 1976
Burgundy, 1978
Brittany, 1979
The French Pyrenees, 1980

also

Walking in France (Oxford Illustrated Press, 1981)

Rob Hunter

Winter Skills

Constable London

First Published in Great Britain 1982
by Constable & Company Ltd
10 Orange Street, London WC2H 7EG
Copyright © 1982 by Robin Hunter Neillands
ISBN 0 09 463900 0
Set in Times New Roman 9pt by
Inforum Ltd, Portsmouth
Printed in Great Britain by
Ebenezer Baylis and Son Ltd
The Trinity Press, Worcester and London

This book is for John and Paul Traynor

Through winter time we call on spring,
And through the spring on summer call,
And when abounding hedges ring,
Declare that winter's best of all.

W. B. Yeats

Acknowledgements

Many people helped with the research for this book, came with me on trips, and were generous with equipment and advice. I would like to say thank you to Paul Traynor of *Practical Camper* for his company in the Pyrenees and Spain; Nigel Gifford of *Mountain World*; Danny Rose and Alan Blackshaw for showing me deep snow techniques at Val d'Isère and Bohinj; the instructors of ski mountain schools at Jackson Hole, Wyoming and Aspen, Colorado; John Traynor for his company in Appalachia; the staff of the Alpine School, Innsbruck and the Alpine School, Salzburg, Austria; Brian Spencer of the Y.H.A., Mike Parsons of Karrimor Ltd; Paul Howcroft of Rohan Ltd; Reg Lumsden of Berghaus Ltd; Maureen Bell of Inghams Travel; Ray Longbottom of 3M Ltd (*Thinsulate*); Reg Popham; Mauricette Manass for help in the Alpes-Maritimes; and as always, to Bunny Percy and Estelle Huxley who can read my writing, and my good friend Terry Brown, for his excellent illustrations.

Rob Hunter, 1981

Contents

Illustrations

Introduction

This is a book about winter. It is designed to follow on from and extend the information contained in my previous book in this series, *The Outdoor Companion*, which covered the basic skills necessary for full enjoyment of land-based outdoor activities in the three main seasons of the year.

The growth of interest in the outdoors has thrived in recent years, to the extent that the popularity of walking, camping and backpacking has, to some extent, deprived the enthusiasts of some of the pleasures they went outdoors to find. People are now walking, camping and backpacking in the most remote parts of the world, and in more populated countries the erosion caused by the passing of many booted feet has been added to the ever-lengthening list of environmental problems.

To escape back into the wild many people are now turning away from the obvious months of spring, summer and autumn, the accepted 'three seasons' of the outdoor world, and exploring the very different world of winter, when the crowds have gone and the wilderness becomes wilderness again.

Winter, however, is not a season for the absolute beginner. It is a time when the balance which exists between man and the elements has tilted in favour of the wild, and when a very small error in technique or a minor inadequacy in equipment can have quite unforeseen consequences. Winter calls for competence in outdoor skills, for good equipment, sound technique, and some experience in the three seasons as the initial grounding.

This book then is about winter in the wild, how to endure it and how to enjoy it. It will first state and thereafter assume a level of three-season competence in the reader, for it is my belief that no one should travel into the winter hills without some practical experience of the same places in summer. This should include:

1. The possession of suitable clothing and equipment plus some experience in using it.

2. Competence with map and compass and their use for hill navigation.
3. A knowledge of weather lore and the ability to interpret forecasts.
4. Competence in first aid.
5. Good physical fitness and experience in three-season outdoor living.
6. A knowledge of survival and rescue techniques.

These subjects were fully detailed in *The Outdoor Companion* and this book starts from the point where these skills have been mastered.

I also want to dispel the idea that winter is a time fraught with hazard. Some books on winter activities approach the entire subject as a survival situation, or go to the other extreme and regard winter activities simply as summer jaunts in woolly underwear. Given a modicum of care and a grasp of specific *winter* skills, in addition to those skills listed above, there is nothing to fear in the cold, snow and ice of winter. It presents a challenge, certainly, but more than that, it's fun.

As with *The Outdoor Companion*, I must declare an interest in the cause of fun. Outdoor activities are undertaken primarily for fun, and one of my objects in writing this book was to enable the reader to get more out of the outdoors. Competence in any activity leads to greater enjoyment, for it enables the activity to be exploited to the full.

Winter itself expands the range of outdoor activities, and to the three-season activities of walking, camping and backpacking we can add cross-country Nordic skiing, ski-mountaineering, snow-shoeing, snow-holing, and work with ice axe and crampons. Winter is the time for travelling in the wild, when fresh skills, fresh challenges and different opportunities are available for the pleasure of the winter traveller.

A book needs a beginning, an end, and limits. This book begins (again) at the point at which three-season skills have been mastered. It stops short of rock-climbing, let alone ice-climbing, and all-out winter expeditions of the trans-Arctic variety, but it does cover shorter one- to three-week winter trips into remote terrain. All such trips need planning, and that, too, is carefully covered.

The book is limited to land-based activities and will, therefore, be useful to those walkers, campers and backpackers of all ages and both sexes who enjoy the outdoors at any time and would like to see more of it. To save repetition of the words 'walker', 'camper' and 'backpacker', I shall frequently refer to them as 'travellers', which has the additional advantage of being neutral to both sex and occupation.

How to use this book

This book should first be read in its entirety, for in winter especially, one item, skill or piece of advice is often directly linked to something else and all must be considered. For its secondary use as a work of reference I must direct you to the index.

To avoid constant repetition of basic points, I have already summarised a level of competence and the advice and comments given relate to that level and aim to extend it. All specific references and recommendations relate to the *winter* use of equipment and activities in cold weather climates, not necessarily in the United Kingdom, and must be accepted from that viewpoint. Specific winter skills recommended conform to accepted current practice, but since outdoor activities are now popular in all parts of the world I have drawn on advice from Canada, the United States, and Continental Europe to supplement and expand the information which is specifically relevant to conditions in the U.K. This, too, is worth remembering.

Standards and opinions on gear and techniques change very quickly in the outdoor world, where last year's gospel is very often this year's heresy. A degree of practical up-to-date research seemed advisable, so in the course of writing this book I visited outdoor establishments and areas in Wales, Scotland, the Alps and Pyrenees, France, Italy, Austria and Spain, Canada, New England, Wyoming, Colorado, Utah and California.

One final point concerns my personal point of view. I resist the pressure to be dogmatic. Winter will swat down anyone who forces his views on her, and the winter traveller must be flexible. A good companion, a Winter Companion, should give good advice, but you alone, out in the winter wild, can judge how and when to apply it. Were I there on the spot, and you asked my advice, I might well say, 'Yes, but . . .'; and so here I have given several views and opinions on many issues if they seem to have some relevance in particular situations. When in doubt, I err on the side of caution, and if this is wrong then so be it, for it stems from the fact that my readers are unknown to me. I hope that no one is ever found dead in the hills with one of my books in his rucksack!

Equipment and clothing

Equipment and clothing for winter use must be manufactured to an adequate standard and suitable for the chosen activity, in any conceivable weather conditions. I have therefore chosen to tackle the subject of clothing and equipment in two ways, firstly by suggesting how three-season equipment may be upgraded for winter use, and secondly by stressing the essential features which should be found in items designed specifically for winter use.

Prices

In this book there is no mention of prices. Prices are constantly increasing and any advice on the subject in a book of this nature could never be accurate. Provided the essential winter features exist in the item in question, it is probably fair to say that you will get the quality you are prepared to pay for, no more and no less, and I must urge you to buy the best you can afford. Winter is no place for shoddy equipment. Current prices for your particular part of the world are best investigated in an up-to-date edition of the your local outdoor magazines, a list of which is given on page 226.

Finally, when referring to the individual I tend to conform to accepted practice and use 'he' as the pronoun. It could equally well be 'she' and indeed must be so, here and there. Winter activities are by no means confined to men and no slight to women is intended by my use of the masculine form.

Some are weather wise, and some are otherwise. . . .

Ben Franklin

Winter is different. Gone are the warm soft days of summer, golden autumns, the green flushes of spring. Winter can be a harsh, bleak, demanding time of year, when life in the countryside retreats, knowing that this is the time to lie low and rest while Nature does its worst. Yet, as a result of these unwelcoming features, winter offers challenges and presents opportunities, demanding in return a different attitude in those who choose to leave behind the more obvious outdoor times and continue on into the uncertain world of winter. Winter can be fun.

To those who know it well the chief attraction of winter is that solitude has returned to the wild. Even the familiar places are exciting. The crowds have gone, the litter and erosion is hidden beneath the snow and summer places become fresh and attractive again when winter has driven away the public and draped the trees with frost and snow. Winter is the time when even a short walk can reveal that this is the time of year when you must be on guard, a period when commonsense, technique and alertness have to be deployed all the time and not just in moments of alarm.

Outdoor people enjoy the winter months for all these reasons and because the very demands of winter call out every skill and faculty, and heighten that sense of adventure which attracted them to the outdoors in the first place.

That apart, winter requires that those who wish to go there safely have a good grasp of basic three-season outdoor techniques as well as a knowledge of specific winter skills. It would be idle to pretend that winter is simply an extension of the other seasons. Winter cold can sap your strength and test your physical and mental abilities to the limit. Moreover, in a head-on contest, man cannot win. Winter is tougher than any human frame, so you must be crafty. Fitness, common sense, a sense of humour and the ability to plan are essential personal qualities in winter and when these are allied to a grasp of winter skills, then the outdoor traveller is the true outdoorsman, able to enjoy the outdoor world in all its moods, summer and winter.

Winter mastery must start with a grasp of three-season skills and a sound knowledge of the weather.

Competence out of doors at any time is based on three main factors:

1. Personal and physical qualities.
2. A command of the necessary skills.
3. Experience.

The first calls for an honest appraisal of personal attitudes, for competence depends more on attitude than on anything else and outdoors, especially in the winter, no personal quality is more important than common sense.

Common sense itself is composed of a cool head, the ability to reason and evaluate facts, and the moral strength to resist impulses and pressures which you *know* to be wrong, or at least inadvisable. Outdoors, common sense – or the lack of it – often reveals itself in the attitude taken by the leader to the weaker members of the party, and in the example he or she gives to others. Along with common sense must go the self-discipline necessary to put it into practice.

Without having common sense, and using it, winter can be an unpleasant place, and – yes – fraught with frequent hazards. But add to common sense the ability to plan and a sense of humour, and winter becomes enjoyable. One very useful personal quality in winter is the ability to get on with others. It is possible, but limiting, to go into the winter world alone. Longer trips require companions, and the group must be compatible, which means that to a greater or lesser extent the members must modify their personal wishes in the interests of the common good.

Winter is not tolerant of petty likes and dislikes, and if there is a

Spring ski-ing in the Swiss Alps

weakness in the individual or the group, winter will find it out. I am not referring here to morality, but integrity and self-awareness. Winter will not let you get away with slipshod preparation, inadequate equipment or a poor plan. Winter demands that you use your head at the start and keep it throughout, no matter what happens.

Physical abilities stem from this, for in winter above all it pays to be fit, and to keep your activities within the limits dictated by that level of competence and fitness. Winter is no time for long rests on sunny banks. In winter it pays to keep moving, for those who move stay warm. In winter those who volunteer for extra tasks, and keep their bodies active, gain in extra warmth and lower exposure risks, but this area too calls for judgement. Fight winter too hard and you will tire first, for there is no end to the resources contained in the elements. It takes brains, technique and experience, not just brute force, to combat the incalculable onslaughts of winter.

If you lack such experience, then to gain experience in the other three seasons of the year is a first essential. Having done so, it is possible to go out into the winter hills with a more experienced friend, who can pass on his skills and show you what to do. Any group needs a balance of resources, but any well-adjusted, experienced companion, even without specific winter experience, is never a drag on the party. In this way experience gets passed on and spread around, providing that the one is willing to teach and the other willing to learn.

The first question to be asked about yourself and your companions is a difficult one, and requires an honest answer. Do you have the personal and physical qualities to face the challenges of winter, squarely and without complaint? If you can give an honest 'Yes' to that, then it's time to look at the weather. The winter cannot be mastered or even given a fair run for its money unless the outdoorsman or woman has a solid grasp of weather lore, and knows in particular how to combat *cold*.

Weather

The first lesson to learn about the weather is that every weather system or climatic state has its problems. Meteorologists describe the weather in Britain as 'temperate', while meteorologists in the northern U.S.A. and Canada admit that their winters are severe, with long periods of deep cold and heavy snowfalls.

Few British mountains exceed 4000 ft (1300 m.) and none has snow all the year round, but British weather is very changeable and all too often damp. In such a situation height is often irrelevant. Britain's mountains are in some ways more dangerous than those of Europe and North America because the British hill-walker and climber has to contend with weather which is fundamentally unreliable and is characterised by rain, sleet, snow, mist and a pervading damp. Dry cold, even at altitude, is not nearly so serious as the damp cold of Britain, especially when allied to wind.

The expression 'temperate weather' can lead the inexperienced outdoorsman to conclude that British hills can be taken for granted, but 'temperate' is a relative phrase, and means simply that in the U.K. and much of Western Europe, the weather is neither very hot nor very cold. It is, however, very changeable and no conditions can be relied on to persist for any length of time.

In the U.S.A. and Canada the winter weather is often very severe. In Alaska, much of Canada and Greenland, temperatures of $-34°C$ ($-30°F$) or even lower are not uncommon in winter. Cold of this intensity is difficult to imagine. Windscreens can shatter, and gas cigarette lighters are useless. Engine oil becomes as thick as butter and petrol freezes in carburettors. Telephone wires snap like string, and touching bare metal rips the skin from your hands. The snow is granular and firm, easily supporting the weight of cars and tractors. In such temperatures the margin of life is a fine one, but at least you know where you are. Long, hard, freezing winters can be confidently anticipated and the worst effects guarded against. The risks truly begin at lesser temperatures and especially in cold, damp, windy weather.

N.A.T.O. troops operating in Norway have very useful guidelines for living outside and moving in deep cold conditions. The ideal temperature is about $-10°C$ ($14°F$). Untrained troops are withdrawn from the field at about $-20°C$ ($-4°F$) and movement of trained troops becomes difficult at $-30°C$ ($-22°F$). The real hazards begin though when the temperature rises to around $-5°C$

(23°F) and the wind gets up. Slush and wet snow dampens tents and clothing and if the wind rises life becomes impossible.

Winter, then, is a variable period, and you must decide if your winter is the deep, extreme, but reliable kind or the milder but more varied and less reliable type. Both can be lethal to the unprepared.

With chilling damp, or cold, wet days, the chief weather hazard to the outdoorsman in winter is the wind, which in combination with such cold introduces the windchill factor.

Windchill

The windchill factor is a simple concept. It is based on the fact that wind will combine with cold to lower the effective air temperature dramatically.

The following chart illustrates the windchill factor and should be studied carefully.

Two things are worth remembering when considering windchill factors. First, that winds over 40 m.p.h. (60 k.p.h.) have little additional effect and, secondly, that good clothing and effective technique in using it can limit the effect of windchill even at very low temperatures. Body heat is often lost by convection, warmth being sucked away from the body by the action of cold air passing over the surface of the garments. It is essential, therefore, that winter garments provide adequate insulation. This will be fully covered in the next chapter.

Estimated Wind Speed in Km. per hr.	Actual Thermometer Reading (°C)											
	10	4	–1	–7	–12	–18	–23	–29	–34	–40	–46	–51
	Equivalent Temperature (°C)											
Calm	10	4	–1	–7	–12	–18	–23	–29	–34	–40	–46	–51
8	9	3	–3	–9	–14	–21	–26	–32	–38	–44	–49	–46
16	4	–2	–9	–16	–23	–29	–36	–43	–50	–57	–64	–71
24	2	–6	–13	–21	–28	–38	–43	–50	–58	–65	–73	–80
32	0	–8	–16	–23	–32	–39	–47	–55	–63	–71	–79	–83
40	–1	–9	–18	–26	–34	–42	–51	–59	–67	–76	–83	–92
48	–2	–11	–19	–28	–36	–44	–53	–62	–70	–78	–87	–96
56	–3	–12	–20	–29	–37	–45	–55	–63	–72	–81	–89	–98
64	–3	–12	–21	–30	–38	–47	–56	–65	–73	–82	–91	–100

Little Danger (for properly clothed person)			Increasing Danger			Great Danger		
			To exposed flesh					

Estimated Windspeed In M.P.H	Actual Thermometer Reading (°F)											
	50	40	30	20	10	0	–10	–20	–30	–40	–50	–60
	Equivalent Temperature (°F)											
Calm	50	40	30	20	10	0	–10	–20	–30	–40	–50	–60
5	48	37	27	16	6	–5	–15	–26	–36	–47	–57	–68
10	40	28	16	4	–9	–21	–33	–46	–58	–70	–83	–95
15	36	22	9	–5	–18	–36	–45	–58	–72	–85	–99	–112
20	32	18	4	–10	–25	–39	–53	–67	–82	–96	–110	–124
25	30	16	0	–15	–29	–44	–59	–74	–88	–104	–118	–133
30	28	13	–2	–18	–33	–48	–63	–79	–94	–109	–125	–140
35	27	11	–4	–20	–35	–49	–67	–82	–98	–113	–129	–145
40	26	10	–6	–21	–37	–53	–69	–85	–100	–116	–132	–148

Little Danger (for properly clothed person			Increasing Danger			Great Danger		
			To exposed flesh					

Temperature lapse rate

Snow on tops

Sleet on slopes

Rain in valley

Winter effects

The three-season walker or camper is well accustomed to the odd
bad day, but may be unable to cope with a succession of them, and
unable to appreciate just how extreme winter can be out of doors
and in the higher hills.

In arctic, sub-zero weather the traveller must cope with the
sapping effects of cold and be wary of the effects of cold on his
immediate environment. Cold metal sticks to the skin, and must
never be touched with the ungloved hand. Frostbite is a constant
possibility, and the use of heavy insulating garments can lead to
dampness from perspiration, which in turn leads to a fresh range of
problems.

Sub-arctic cold, at around the 0°C level, comes into the unreliable
area. With the damp comes the possibility of hypothermia, and the
problems caused by rain, mist and fog, of which poor visibility and
unsafe ice-covered paths are just two.

Winter cold is compounded by the fact that air cools with altitude.
Cold air temperatures decline at the rate of 3°C (5.5°F) for every
300 m. (1000 ft) of altitude. This is known as the *temperature lapse
rate*, and while the rate of cooling for warmer air is slightly less, the
effect is that a soft rain in the valleys can be freezing hail or even
snow on the tops, a fact which winter travellers, viewing the weather
through a café window, often fail to realise.

Wind speeds are also higher on upper slopes, owing to increased
exposure and the absence of trees, and this increases the windchill
factor.

During the winter months we experience more of the unpleasant
side of weather, and meet weather effects which are unknown or
uncommon in summer. Low cloud, mist and fog can and do blanket
the hills for days on end. Snow can fall even when the temperature
is well above zero, but there is little truth in the saying that it is 'too
cold for snow'. Snowfalls occur down to −30°C (−22°F), and bring
with them blizzards, which will swirl into the smallest gap in tent
door or clothing zip; deep snow, which will block routes and cause
avalanches; as well as ice and 'white-outs' when snow and mist
merge into one grey mass.

The winter outdoorsman cannot avoid these effects. They are

part of winter and must be anticipated. His attitude and equipment must be designed to cope with them, and the weather forecast is one of the winter outdoorsman's most useful allies.

Weather forecasts

It is clear from all this that in coping with winter, whether it is the damp and variable kind familiar to the British, or the severe sort found in the Americas, prevention is better than cure. The winter outdoorsman must obtain weather forecasts regularly and be able to interpret them.

I have included a grasp of weather lore as an essential outdoor skill. It is useful in any season but vital in winter.

Every nation in the world produces and circulates weather information. It is provided primarily for those who live and work out of doors, for fishermen and farmers, for pilots in the air and ships at sea, but such information is readily available to outdoor people and must be obtained, interpreted and understood by the winter traveller.

Official forecasts can be obtained in four ways: from the Press, from television, from radio, and by direct application to a weather (met.) centre.

Weather Centre

Contacting a weather centre will result in the most up-to-date forecast. The telephone numbers of local weather stations can be found in the Yellow Pages of most telephone directories. Weather stations are frequently found on airfields, and even if no weather station is mentioned a phone call to the control tower of the local civil airfield will usually provide a reliable forecast. The airfield authorities are bound to provide such forecasts to aircraft, and are always willing to help outdoor people.

The press

Newspapers give very general forecasts, and because the information has to be gathered, printed and distributed, it is bound to be a little out of date. On the other hand the forecasts cover wide areas, and if collated over several days they give a good idea of current weather patterns.

Television and radio
Television forecasts are excellent, cover wide areas, and improve steadily with the growing use of satellite pictures which show weather trends. In North America, weather forecast presentation has become almost a part of show business, and the forecasts, while gaining in artistic impact, fall down on technical merit. Radio forecasts, especially the shipping forecasts, are often excellent. Outdoor people should be particularly interested in those provided by local radio stations in hill and mountain areas, as a service to residents and visitors. Weather is always subject to local variation and a local forecast is always worth obtaining. Broadcast times are published in the local papers.

Section through a depression showing cold and warm fronts

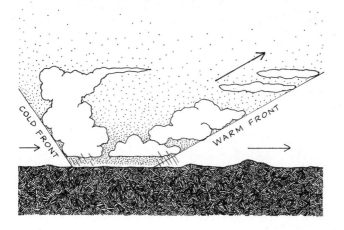

Other sources
Other sources are the Police or Park Rangers, Mountain Centres, or even the local outdoor shop, where the staff can often tell you what to expect just by glancing out of the window.

Preparing your forecast
To some degree all forecasts are general forecasts, in the sense that no published forecast is designed to match your particular requirements. To obtain a forecast relevant to your plans or situation you must interpret the weather information and prepare a forecast plan of your own.

Using the most up-to-date information for the area concerned, which is usually noted from the radio or obtained by telephone from the weather station, the outdoor person needs information on the following points:

1. Date and time the forecast was issued.
2. Period covered.
3. Practical information on pressure, temperature, precipitation, visibility and wind speed.
4. Approach of warm or cold fronts.
5. Any predictions on weather behaviour *beyond* the forecast period. ·
6. Any local variations.

Before going out in the winter hills, the outdoorsman must be able to interpret this information, and make an accurate prediction for the area he or she is in, or is about to enter, and for a foreseeable period ahead. This task can be allotted to some party member otherwise inexperienced in winter. He or she may not yet know how to fit crampons or use an ice axe, but can, by providing an accurate relevant forecast, make a significant contribution to the success and well-being of the group.

Updating the forecast
A study of weather trends for a few days before the start, plus local information and advice, will get the trip off to a good start, but all

weather information must be regularly updated.

Radios are often carried for this purpose, and to while away those long dark nights, but reception is often poor in the hills, even if you remember to protect the batteries from cold and note down the times when forecasts are broadcast. Information should be gleaned from other parties, by dropping into huts and hostels, and by observing weather signs generally, especially cloud cover. Note the prevailing wind and beware of lowering cloud and the presence of *stratus* and *nimbo-stratus* clouds, which usually precede bad weather.

Cumulonimbus clouds

Pressure is the most reliable guide to changes in the weather, and a regular noting of pressure variations is advisable on any extended trip. This requires that the group should possess a barometer. Lightweight pocket barometers are now available, and recording the pressure reading at any stop will provide a useful guide to changes in the weather. It is necessary to adjust the barometer for height, since as you climb pressure falls. Normal 'sea-level' pressure is 1013 millibars, and it falls about 30 millibars for every 300 metres you climb, a fact which must be taken into account when reading the barometer in the hills. Check your height from the map, and adjust the barometers accordingly. If the pressure is noted down four times a day, at three-hourly intervals, the information can be noted and changes allowed for in your plans.

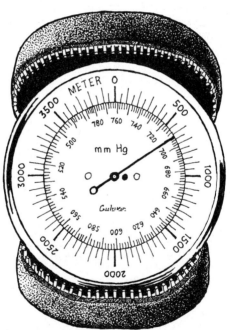

A pocket altimeter/barometer

Prevention

To restate the obvious is often necessary, and I intend to do so often in this book. Remember, when coping with winter weather, that prevention is better than any known cure. An analysis by the *Commission on Accident Prevention* revealed that exposure problems in winter are often due to the following causes:

1. *Inadequate Clothing*: People persist in going on to the hill in flimsy anoraks and jeans. However, the report states that even the correct clothing is useless if it is wet, so good clothing *and* the technique to keep it dry are both required.
2. *Poor Technique*: A number of actions can be put under this heading, particularly failure to recognise exposure symptoms in the early stages (page 170). It is also inadvisable for inexperienced people to go into the mountains alone and dangerous for parties to press on at all costs in poor weather instead of seeking shelter while still warm and dry. Exercise in sodden garments causes rapid loss of body heat.

3. *Ignorance and Stupidity*: People fail to realise just how deadly a wet, cold day on a hill or mountain can be, and refuse to be told. This comment holds good even for leaders of organised parties and school groups, who often have no mountain training and all too frequently lack the wit to appreciate that the winter hills are a different place from the school sports field.

Precautions

To combat all but the last item, against which the gods themselves labour in vain, the following actions will usually be adequate:

1. Make a plan which reflects the ability of the group and stick to it.
2. Wear or carry warm and windproof clothing, including gloves and headgear.
3. Be aware of the threat, symptoms and prevention of exposure/hypothermia.
4. Seek shelter directly anyone weakens far from base.
5. Stay together to preserve warmth and companionship.
6. Leave a route card behind, just in case.

Some of these subjects have been touched on already, and all will be explained in detail in the course of this book.

The objects of this chapter can be summarised as follows:

1. To state the importance of a firm grasp of three-season outdoor skills before tackling the hills in winter.
2. To emphasise the importance of personal qualities — common sense, fitness and consideration for others — in the face of winter's challenge.
3. To stress and restress that the prime factor in winter is the weather. The weather must be understood, resisted and, perhaps, endured.

A list of books covering weather lore in considerable detail is given in the bibliography, and all readers of this book are urged to consult them and know them thoroughly.

Finally though, winter is *not* a place of danger and death and pain. It is clean, fresh, exciting and alive. Every problem has some compensating advantage, and if the problems are recognised and accepted as part of the challenge they can be readily overcome, or avoided.

Ski touring in Norway

2·Winter Clothing

Beware of all enterprises that require new clothes

H. D. Thoreau

In summer, the correct clothing is important. In winter, the correct clothing is essential. In summer it is possible, if not always enjoyable, to wear any old comfortable clothes, and accept the occasional soaking as just part of the game. In winter a soaking can be a serious matter, and just any old clothes won't do.

The selection of correct wear for winter is governed by what is known as the 'layer principle', based on the fact that several thin layers of clothing are warmer than one thick layer. This is due to the insulation value of the 'dead' or still air trapped between the layers. This principle underpins much of the thinking that goes into the manufacture of garments and the fillings they contain, as well as the way in which experienced outdoor people dress in winter.

The problem
In winter the main enemies to comfort and survival outdoors are:

1. Wind.
2. Precipitation (rain, snow, sleet, etc.).
3. Cold.
4. Damp (from mist, melted snow, perspiration).
5. Perspiration.
6. Any combination of the above.

We have already discussed the effects of wind, cold and damp and their effects have been quantified by the windchill factor. Perspiration is worth stressing, for any activity in winter clothes produces heat and sweat. Essentially, the well-clad outdoorsman is safe, even in a cold climate, provided he can stay dry. Rain soaking through garments, or damp from any other cause, gradually and imperceptibly reduces the insulating value of your clothing, and will destroy the margins of comfort and safety. Add a little wind to the damp, and a drop in temperature, and there could be a problem.

Moreover – and this is a fact which is often overlooked – garments can lose insulation from perspiration just as easily as from rain and snow. Perspiration is just as much a problem as precipitation and a good deal more difficult to combat. These, then, are the problems, and the answers are found in a combination of science and technique.

The solution

A major part of the answer is provided by suitable clothing; and suitable clothing is based upon the layer principle, which depends on the ability of garments, or their filling, to trap and hold air, and thus provide insulation.

This ability has now been quantified and the insulation value of garments is measured in *clo's*. One *clo* represents the insulation value of a light business suit, and in the outdoors one *clo* of insulation is rarely enough.

Scientific tests were recently carried out on a number of exposure victims. They were wearing boots, stockings, jeans, cotton underwear, string vest, wool shirt and pullover, and an anorak (parka) with a hood; in other words, fairly typical outdoor clothing for summer use, and good enough if the weather stayed mild and the wearer kept moving. Tests proved that these garments when dry had an insulation value of 1.8 *clo*, but when wet and exposed to a mild 16 k.p.h. (10 m.p.h.) wind, the *clo* rating fell to .17. They might as well have been naked.

Outdoors in winter calls for good clothing, worn in layers, with an adequate *clo* value. Sleeping at say −34°C (−30°F) you would need up to 12 *clo*, but if you are *moving* at such a temperature, 4 *clo* would be adequate.

At −18°C (0°F) a 7-*clo* bag will keep a man warm for hours, while for someone on the move 2-3 *clo* is adequate. Much depends on the way such clothing is used, for the inbuilt *clo* values will be reduced if the garments become saturated by rain, snow or perspiration.

I have found 2-*clo*-rated garments very warm indeed for winter hill walking, and 4-*clo* too cold for downhill skiing. However, just having some yardstick to measure the combined insulation effect of filling, materials and design in garments must be beneficial, and we can only hope that *clo* ratings are increasingly included in garment tags.

Garment materials

Winter garment shells are usually made from synthetics, like nylon or helenca, or polycotton blends. Ideally all winter garments should breathe to let body heat evaporate, and should definitely not seal off the body and cause excessive perspiration. Rip-stop nylon fabric, laced with thread to stop tears spreading, is a useful skin for anoraks, but beware of overheating. Stretch 'helenca' fabric is good for trousers and breeches, for it is warm and snow-shedding. Polycotton is never more than showerproof and needs reinforcement in wet weather. Gore-Tex is increasingly popular and very effective but still somewhat expensive.

Garment filling

In the beginning there was down, usually duck or goose down. Down provides the perfect filling for outdoor garments and sleeping bags, because the feathers provide lots of that excellent insulator, still, dry air. However, there is a bad fairy at this particular feast, for down is useless if it gets wet. The feathers clog together, so the insulation is lost.

Down is light, very warm and highly compressible but 'lofts' or expands well to provide dead air and is widely used in situations of reliable below-zero temperatures, or in combination with waterproof shell garments. In the often rainy, moist weather of Northern Europe and the Western U.S.A., down is not the ideal filling. I have a down jacket and I use it regularly for skiing and for short weekend trips. I know that if the weather turns really foul it is impossible in the end to keep garments dry, so on longer trips I use a garment with a synthetic filling. Besides, down is increasingly expensive.

Synthetic fillings are also based on the dead air principle and employ multi-filament chopped or continuous synthetic products, branded with such names as Hollofil, Thinsulate and so on. The great advantage of these fillings is that even when they get wet they still provide insulation because the fibres do not matt together as down does. To be quite accurate, no filling provides insulation as such. It is the 'dead air' spaces which the filling produces which provide the insulation, and the more 'dead air' there is, the warmer the garment. Hollofil is bulkier than Thinsulate, and harder to pack into a rucksack but Hollofil is also less compressible and therefore better for use in sleeping bags.

Fibre-pile is another popular insulator in more temperate regions, and is very popular with walkers and skiers. Pile is a teased-out fabric made from a single synthetic fibre or a wool-synthetic blend. Fibre-pile garments are comfortable and conform well to the body, but offer little resistance to a keen wind and need reinforcing with, say, a down vest. I use a fibre-pile jacket and sleeveless down vest for cross-country skiing and it is an excellent combination. Wool is rarely used as a filling but can always provide an extra layer since, unlike cotton, wool gives a considerable amount of warmth even when wet.

It may seem that the best choice for winter is a garment or sleeping bag with a synthetic filling such as Hollofil or Thinsulate, and that down, which is expensive anyway, could be allowed to pass quietly out of use. However, synthetic fillings have their snags. They are still not as warm as down, weight for weight, and are often bulky, stiff to wear and difficult to pack. The choice depends on the climate, the activity intended and the finance available. Good clothes are not cheap, and apart from the filling it is the design and construction of the garment which provides the insulation.

Garment manufacture

Heat is drawn from the body in four ways:

1. Convection.
2. Conduction.
3. Evaporation.
4. Radiation.

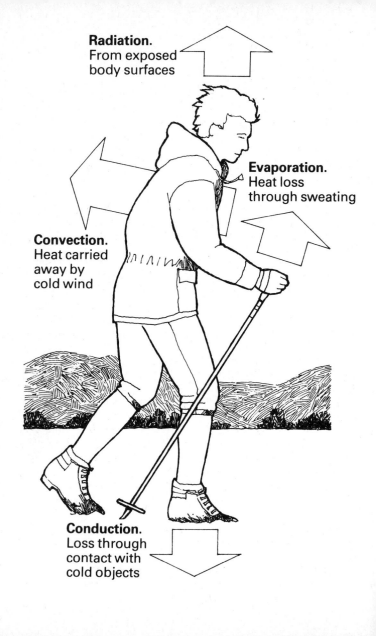

Radiation. From exposed body surfaces

Evaporation. Heat loss through sweating

Convection. Heat carried away by cold wind

Conduction. Loss through contact with cold objects

Heat loss is caused by convection when warm air near the body is carried away by a cold wind, or by the 'bellows' effect of badly fitting garments. Steady convection heat loss leads to trouble from windchill, but can be reduced by wearing windproof layer clothing which fits well. You must keep the cold air out and the warmed body air in. Ill-fitting garments, unsecured at neck, wrists and waist, pump out the warm air and suck in the cold. The body can lose up to 50% of the heat it generates in this way, and it is essential that your winter clothing is snug fitting and capable of sealing in the air at neck and wrists.

Evaporation is, not to put too fine a point on it, sweat. The body is constantly producing perspiration, and if you are to retain insulation in winter heat loss through evaporation must be controlled, sweating minimised and the damping effect of perspiration on the clothing at least reduced. Here again, garment construction is vital. Garments need full-length zips, and need to be of breathable fabrics. Waterproofed garments simply encourage perspiration to build up inside the clothing which, as a result, loses insulation. Early arctic explorers, using unsuitable garments which did not allow body heat to evaporate, found that they froze solid when soaked with sweat. Be sure your garments have good zips, and use the zips regularly to reduce body heat, and the inevitable perspiration, to the absolute minimum.

Conduction heat loss is caused by contact with cold objects and is greater when the filling of a garment is inadequate in either quantity or quality and the garment is of inferior manufacture. If a filling is compressed against a cold surface, say when lying in your sleeping bag on the bare ground, heat will be drawn away. A thin sleeping mat or pad chilled by the ground is not adequate additional protection. In winter, your socks will, when compressed by your weight, lose insulation and lead to cold feet. Touching the chill metal of ice axes, stoves or tent pegs also causes conductive heat loss.

Radiated heat escapes from all exposed body surfaces, such as your head. If you are cold, put your hat on. If you are too warm, take it off.

Garments must be designed and manufactured to minimise heat

loss from these four causes and *used* by the wearer in such a way as to dispel body heat and retain adequate warmth. The garment cannot do it alone.

Let me summarise the points so far:

1. The principle to observe for winter warmth in clothing is the layer principle.
2. Dead air space – not just the material which provides it – is the main weapon against winter cold and wind.
3. Garments must be chosen to match the climatic conditions most commonly encountered in your part of the world, dry cold or wet cold.
4. Garment construction and use is as important as the materials used in manufacture.

If these four points are remembered and applied, the winter outdoorsman will be dressed to beat off the worst of winter's rages, in suitable clothing, well fitted, well filled, and correctly used.

Upgrading three-season wear

In countries with a temperate climate where the summers are not so hot or the winters too cold, special winter garments may not be entirely necessary, except perhaps for a heavier weight cagoule or some synthetic-filled outer garments to cope with wet-cold conditions.

In such areas, a few extra items, or the addition of an extra layer of insulation to normal three-season clothing, may be all that is usually required. Considering these extras will also enable us to think of ways in which even specially designed winter garments can receive that little extra support if, in the event, they turn out to be not *quite* warm enough for the conditions we encounter on the hill.

Boots

If they are roomy enough, wear an extra pair of thin socks, or insert neoprene or even paper insoles. Proof the boots against wet, especially in the welt and along the seams.

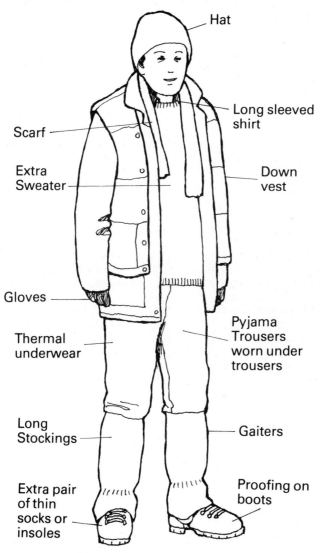

Hat

Long sleeved shirt

Scarf

Down vest

Extra Sweater

Gloves

Thermal underwear

Pyjama Trousers worn under trousers

Long Stockings

Gaiters

Extra pair of thin socks or insoles

Proofing on boots

Upgrading 3 season wear

Insoles
Insoles are useful, especially if you are wearing crampons, which, being metal, can cause conductive heat loss. Neoprene insoles, cut from an old wet-suit, are excellent.

Stockings
Carry several spare pairs, and wear long gaiters. Loop-stitched socks are very warm and comfortable at any time but especially so in winter.

Trousers or breeches
A pair of pyjama trousers worn under trousers greatly increases insulation and can even be worn with breeches, without looking odd, if long stockings are pulled up over the lower legs!

Shirts and sweaters
Wear long-sleeved shirts. An extra sweater will increase insulation considerably. Be sure that the shirt is well tucked in and close the neck and cuffs securely. Wear a scarf.

Underwear
Thermal underwear, top and long-johns, will not only increase insulation but also act like a wick to draw any perspiration from the body.

Hat and gloves
The head is the body's radiator. Keep it covered to stay warm or bare the head to keep cool. Protect the ears. Gloves should have long cuffs to cover the wrists where the blood flows close to the surface. Mittens are warmer than gloves. Wearing a pair of silk inner gloves is also a good idea. In cold conditions always carry spare gloves.

Outer garments
A down vest or waistcoat worn on top of a fibre-pile jacket gives good extra insulation. The vest can upgrade a summertime fibre-pile jacket into one adequate for ski-touring or snow-shoeing.

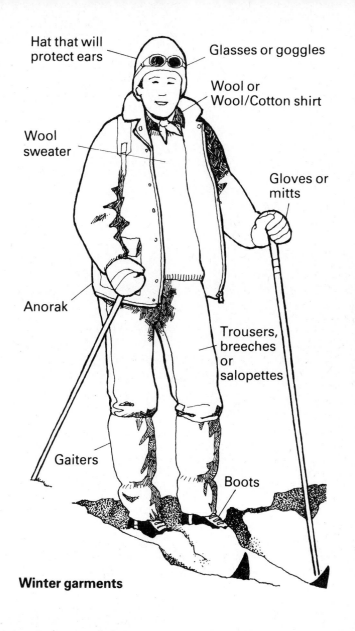

Hat that will protect ears

Glasses or goggles

Wool or Wool/Cotton shirt

Wool sweater

Gloves or mitts

Anorak

Trousers, breeches or salopettes

Gaiters

Boots

Winter garments

Many outer garments work all the better in winter if the seams are sealed with some suitable spray. These sprays are usually silicone based and help to prevent seams from leaking. Check with your supplier for a preparation which suits your particular garment.

Wearing these extra items of clothing can upgrade your existing range of clothing to an adequate winter level at little extra cost. Remember, though, the effect of perspiration. Winter garments must have zips and winter walkers must use them. Just swaddling yourself in extra layers, without the means to air the body, will lead to overheating, sweating and heat loss.

Winter garments

Thanks to the effect of design and fashion on the outdoor clothing scene, most – but not all – garments contain winter features. Unfortunately some of the features are included purely for cosmetic purposes and not for serious use. A rucksack which has ice-axe loops but no crampon-patch or laces is a good example of cosmetic production, for if you need to carry an ice axe you ought to take crampons.

Much of today's outdoor equipment and clothing has been originally designed for and used on high-range 'extreme' expeditions. Outdoor people following more relaxed pursuits get the benefits but can pay a high price for features they may not need. I intend here to list desirable winter features for non-extreme expedition work. If your garments have most of these features you will be adequately protected.

Boots

Winter boots should have speed-lacing hooks, a double sewn-in tongue and as few seams as possible on the upper, and be stiff enough to wear with crampons and give good support on rough ground. Light boots are not suitable in winter. Have boots which can be unlaced and opened out wide to put on, for they will certainly get wet during the day and sooner or later freeze at night. Forcing your feet into frozen boots is hard work. Try hard to keep your boots dry. Gaiters help in this and are essential in winter. You can dry the boots out a little after you take them off at night.

Ski-mountaineering boot

Remember to take them into the tent, and place them somewhere out of the cold air – even in your sleeping bag if need be. I put mine into a stuff-sack, wrap that in spare clothing and use them as a pillow. Use inner-soles and have a spare pair. Do not lace the boots too tightly, or wear so many extra socks that you inhibit circulation, for that could lead to frostbite. The best boots are still leather, and therefore increasingly expensive. Plastic upper boots are coming on to the market and may prove useful in winter, if the inner boot is filled with synthetic.

Rubber-cleated boot soles pack with snow or mud and are useless on ice. You must have crampons. I fell hard into the rocks of a frozen stream a second after stepping out of the tent last winter, so I speak from sharp – even bruised – experience. Boots should be treated with a proofing compound like *Sno-seal* or *Nikwax*, especially in the welt and along the seams, but don't overdo it, a light dressing is enough; completely sealing the boot leads to perspiration inside.

Snow boots

The boots described in the last section are basically three-season boots with winter features. In the deep cold conditions found in the arctic and sub-arctic, a different type of boot is recommended – the *mukluk* or *shoepac*. This is a long calf-length boot, with double tongue and leather uppers, but with a rubber or compound foot and sole, to exclude damp and wetness for deep snow. The mukluk is a compromise between a leather boot and a rubber boot, and aims to exclude damp without creating interior perspiration, which is just as bad. They are warm and comfortable and need to be worn with two pairs of stockings; the stockings need to be changed often, for perspiration is a problem.

Moon-boots, filled with plastic foam, are no good for travelling, but warm to wear at base or around a campsite.

Special footwear for camp wear and cross-country skiing will be covered later.

Stockings

For winter it has to be long stockings, although I wear a pair of short socks as well when on a cross-country ski trip. Both are of loop-stitched construction. I carry several spare pairs of socks, tucked in every corner of my rucksack. Wet socks have no place on your feet in winter, and when all the socks are wet it is time to seek shelter and dry them out. Keep at least one dry pair to wear at night in the sleeping bag.

Winter boots: (From top left to bottom right): Moon boot; cross country ski boot; Alpine boot; ski mountaineering boot; walking boot; down bootees

Underwear

Thermal underwear is a boon in winter. There are light suits in various weights, offering different amounts of insulation, but the following benefits are common to all:

1. Thermal underwear provides an extra layer and is comfortable.
2. It draws away perspiration from the skin, acting like a wick.
3. It is extremely light, compact and easy to carry.

For all these reasons I recommend wearing thermal underwear in winter. In fact I carry two suits, one for wear in the day and one for sleeping in. It is warm even when wet and dries easily. String vests and longjohns are available, but I find them uncomfortable, and think thermal underwear more practical.

Shirts

Wool is the best material, and cotton is frequently condemned, but a shirt of 55% wool and 45% cotton is just about perfect. I like a long-sleeved, long-tailed shirt for walking and camp wear, but I frequently wear a cotton tee-shirt for cross-country skiing. These get wet from perspiration but they dry easily and I can carry several and change them regularly. Upgrade the cotton tee-shirt with a sweater or a wind-shirt, and you can keep your warm wool shirt for wearing at night. I also wear a cotton neckerchief and, if I am going high, carry or wear a scarf.

Hats

Hats are useful, indeed essential in winter to protect the ears and prevent heat loss from the head. I would regard losing my hat as a serious matter.

The received doctrine for hats says that the ideal headgear is the balaclava helmet, which can be worn rolled up or pulled down to protect the ears, cheeks and neck. Quite true, but I find wool balaclavas infernally itchy. If you don't mind that, wear one by all means, but if you do mind, a ski hat, long enough to protect the ears and tight enough to hold your sunglasses in place while skiing, is an adequate substitute. Silk balaclavas are now available, light, very warm, kind to the skin, but expensive. A spare hat is useful.

Gloves or mitts

Here again the choice is yours. I prefer gloves, but ski gloves are not ideal for winter walking, in spite of the useful feature of a long cuff. Walking one winter in the Pyrenees my ski gloves filled up inexorably with water, and froze under my sleeping bag each night. I still use them, *faute de mieux*, but in very cold conditions a pair of long-cuffed Polarguard or Thinsulate-filled mitts might well be warmer and more effective. Losing gloves is a serious matter in sub-zero conditions, so run a tape from each cuff and thread them down your sleeves closing the cuff tightly against rain or snow with velcro tabs. Wearing such 'danglers' may extract a few laughs from friends, but you won't lose your gloves, and the hands will be free to fiddle with compass or cooker. A pair of silk inner gloves to wear when handling metal is useful, and one good idea is to carry a pair of extra large rubber gloves which, pulled on *over* the gloves, can be used for handling liquids, washing-up, etc.

Trousers, breeches, salopettes

Of the first two I prefer trousers, but it is a personal choice. The important features are that the garment should be warm and comfortable, shed snow, not be too tight, and have good deep pockets. The hip and side pockets should be sealed with velcro or button-down tapes. A double seat is vital in winter pants. Zips on the fly can be a problem, for zips can jam. Breeches need to secure well over the knee, covering the stocking tops without gaps. They should be self-supporting or worn with braces, for a belt restricts the garment and loses insulation. In recent years I have taken to wearing salopettes, in a bibbed-and-breeches garment from Rohan, made in a stretch 'helenca' fabric, which sheds snow, is comfortable, has numerous zipped pockets and a useful full-length two-way zip on the fly, and is cut high enough at the back to cover the kidneys. I would recommend salopettes for winter use.

Sweaters

Two light sweaters are warmer than a thick heavy one in ribbed oiled wool, besides being more adaptable and easier to pack. Wool is the ideal material and a light, long-sleeved lambswool sweater will always have a place in my winter pack.

Anoraks (parkas)

Probably the most important and certainly the most expensive purchase you can make is a good winter anorak.

We have already covered the importance of suitable insulation, achieved by correct filling and careful manufacture. Let us now look at the features which a winter jacket should possess. The more it has of these the better the jacket will be.

It should have a large insulated hood with a wired face-piece. The filling should be adequate, well distributed throughout the jacket, and correct for the climate. It should be cut long enough to cover the hips, have inside pockets, and a full-length double zip, which can be opened from the top or the bottom. This zip should be protected with a wide flap secured with press-studs or velcro. The pockets

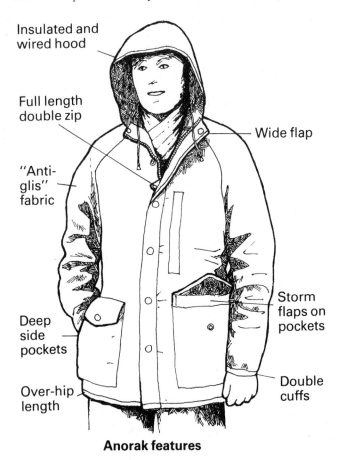

Insulated and wired hood

Full length double zip

Wide flap

"Anti-glis" fabric

Deep side pockets

Storm flaps on pockets

Over-hip length

Double cuffs

Anorak features

should have storm flaps and wide velcro or press-stud-secured outer flaps. Storm flaps are a manufacturing feature in which, when the outer flap is pressed over, the opening of the pocket inside folds down to completely seal the aperture. Deep side hand-warmer pockets, with internal storm flaps, are also useful. The jacket should have double cuffs and be of a breathable *'anti-glis'* fabric, which is not so slippery that a fall means a long slide. The garment should be well made, fit snugly, and be washable, or capable of dry cleaning.

Vests
Sleeveless vests or waistcoats, filled with down or synthetic material or made from fibre-pile, are very useful, and if they have zip-out sleeves are even more adaptable for various climatic conditions.

Jackets
There are those who swear by long jackets in closely woven cotton, with a quilted lining. This sort of garment is popular with wildfowlers and hunters, but lacks the versatility needed by walkers or backpackers, apart from being difficult to pack. They are, however, useful for day walking.

Face masks
Face masks are an occasional item but useful in winter when sub-zero winds are blowing. They need to be used with a good lip salve or barrier cream and help to keep the face from getting chapped or frost-nipped. Face masks come in various fabrics from silk to chamois leather, but silk is warm, light and comfortable. All masks get wet around the mouth from breath condensation and need a cotton breath patch. In some parts of the U.S.A. it is more common, and very effective, to simply cover the lower face with a neckerchief, tied 'outlaw' fashion over the nose and mouth. The condensation from the breath freezes on the neckerchief, but the face within stays warm.

Glasses and goggles
The only real rule for glasses is to carry a spare pair, especially if you have and need glasses with prescription lenses. Sunglasses are

useful in winter, for the glare off the snow can cause headaches, eyestrain, and even snow blindness. They should be dark-tinted and fit closely to the eyes. Side-pieces help to exclude light and are therefore recommended. Secure them against loss by tucking the earpieces under your hat, or tying them behind the head with a cord. Contact lenses are much better than spectacles in winter.

For cross-country skiing, proper ski-goggles are particularly useful on a tour and help to protect the face from frost-nip in low temperatures. One problem with both glasses and goggles is that they tend to fog up, and need constant wiping. A small bottle of 'fog-compound' can be carried, and a wipe of the lenses with this will keep them clear for hours.

Shell clothing
In winter, windproof 'shell clothing' is essential and should be carried all the time. This usually consists of a cagoule (or 'cag'), a pair of over-trousers and long gaiters. Cagoules are slipped on over the head and do impede body ventilation. Cagoules (the word is French and simply means 'hood'), are therefore now being replaced by long front-opening jackets. The shell jacket should have a hood, preferably with a wired face-piece, a full-length front zip covered with a velcro or press-stud-secured flap, and double cuffs. A waist and hem cord can be useful in the wind. The over-trousers should be baggy and gussetted, so that they can be put on over boots. Some walkers have over-trousers which unzip completely at the side, or wear 'wind-chaps' which slip over the legs only.

Gaiters are useful even in summer and essential in winter for they keep wet and mud off boots and stockings, while helping to increase insulation for the feet. Knee-length gaiters with covered zips are ideal.

Ponchos remain popular in the U.S.A., but are rather impractical. They cannot really be worn with a pack, billow about in the wind, and even if they keep out rain, give little protection from windchill.

For winter use, the shell clothing, or certainly the 'cag', should be in heavy duty nylon, coated with neoprene or polyurethane.

The problem with shell clothing is that, while it is worn to keep you dry and prevent wind and wet chill from exterior precipitation, its use greatly increases the risk of condensation. What keeps the cold out keeps body heat in, and this leads to perspiration condensing on the inside of the jacket and dampening the clothing.

The answer to this is to wear as little of the shell clothing as possible, open up the zips as much as you can and reduce your pace to a crawl, thus also reducing the production of body heat.

Another answer is in the development of 'breathable' materials, which permit body heat to disperse. One product, *Gore-Tex*, has been available for some years now and, married to good manufacture, has certainly done a great deal to reduce condensation problems, while still not eliminating them. Basically *Gore-Tex* material is a microporous fabric with minute holes in the surface, large enough to allow the body vapour to escape but small enough to exclude rain droplets. *Gore-Tex* fabric has now been made up into tents, sleeping-bag outers and an increasing range of garments, but its main use is in shell clothing. I have used a *Gore-Tex Mistral* suit from Berghaus for a number of years and would recommend it.

Windshirts and pants
It is often forgotten, especially by those who live in the moist climes of Northern Europe, that the main purpose of shell clothing is to keep the wind out. Those who don't like the clamminess of the full shell suit can settle for a 'windshirt', which is a baggy *blouson* nylon jacket. This is designed to be worn over light inner garments, just to keep the wind out. Wind pants are also available. Such garments are too slight for touring or back country expeditions, but when the wind gets up on a day out they can be useful.

Spare clothing
One of the snags in winter is that you are almost bound to get wet. Sooner or later you will be damp anyway from perspiration. While you are on the move and 'wet-warm' this is no real problem, but when you stop, chill down and become 'wet-cold', hypothermia is a possibility. It is therefore necessary to carry spare clothing. Perhaps I should make it clear that most of the garments discussed in this chapter are really 'spare' clothing for most of the time. The human body is a great engine, producing lots of heat, and while you are on

the move the fewer garments you wear (providing you have adequate protection) the better you will be .

My spare clothing consists of lots of spare socks, a dry set of *Lifa* underwear, spare gloves, and usually a spare tee-shirt, sweater and a scarf. I also carry light moccasins or down bootees to wear in the tent or hut. The other clothing is designed to be used at different times of the day and is spare only until it is needed. When most of this clothing gets wet it is time to find somewhere warm and dry it out. Protect your dry clothing against the wet by keeping it in plastic bags or a stuff-sack.

In recent years we have usually taken one stuff-sack full of dry clothing which we leave at base or in the car boot (trunk) until we return. Having fresh, dry clothes to travel home in is a real boon.

Specialised items
In addition to this fairly normal range of outdoor clothing there are a number of specialised items which may be acquired but need only be used in winter if the weather is exceptionally evil.

Camp boots
Down bootees, made of rip-stop nylon, filled with synthetic and having a chamois sole, are warm and useful for wearing in the tent and for any necessary nocturnal excursions. Even better are moon-boots, high foam-filled boots, very popular as *aprés ski* wear by downhill skiers. The only snag is that moon-boots, while warm, are very bulky, but they are quite light and I have carried a pair strapped to the sides of the sack by the compression straps. The catalogue I have before me even offers electric socks, heated by battery power!

There is no end to the amount of clothing you could take but weight sees to it that only essential items are carried.

Repairs
Good winter clothing is expensive and subjected to hard wear, so it is worth looking after it. Take with you a small repair kit containing 'rip-stop' tape, some safety pins, a needle and thread, as a group item on any long trip. A jammed zip can lead to problems, while a

torn garment leaking down rapidly becomes useless. Clothing which is wet or damp with sweat also loses insulation and needs to be washed out and carefully dried.

Wearing winter clothes

It cannot be emphasised enough that to enjoy the winter world and venture into it safely, a combination of equipment and technique is required.

Good clothing alone is not enough, for if it is not worn properly and used efficiently, it will not protect you.

1. All garments should fit well.
2. Wear no more clothes at any one time than you actually need.
3. Aim to stay no more than comfortably warm and use the zips to ventilate the body and minimise dampness from perspiration.
4. Put on shell clothing in good time. Don't wait to get wet.
5. Brush off snow before it melts.
6. Protect the extremities, head, hands and feet.

It is also necessary to remember that winter, while frequently – indeed usually – is quite a pleasant time if you are used to it, can turn remarkably intolerant to the careless.

Place your clothes where you can get at them. Put on extra garments *before* you become too cold. Think!

After a while all this becomes instinctive, the constant adjusting of zips, the pulling on or taking off of hats, the changing of garments becomes accepted. But that comes with experience, and experience, be it remembered, has been well described as 'One year learning the lessons and many years repeating the mistakes!'

A little neglect may breed much mischief

Ben Franklin

As for clothing, so for equipment. The problems are the same, poor weather, cold and wind, and the requirements in gear are therefore good insulation and efficient performance.

In recent years, outdoor equipment has been manufactured to standards which make much three-season gear perfectly adequate in all but the most severe winter weather; but, as with clothing, a few additional items, a little adaptation here and there, and good technique can ensure adequate comfort and protection at quite a modest additional cost, even when the weather takes a turn for the worse.

Winter equipment proper, designed and manufactured to tackle winter's worst rages head on, does of necessity need special features, which we will examine item by item, but throughout this chapter we must relate all the equipment to groups.

Groups
Winter is the time for outdoor activities in groups. It is, of course, perfectly possible to go walking, backpacking, or ski-touring in winter on one's own. I have done it, and it's good fun, but to go anywhere remote, or to stay out in the winter wild for much longer than a weekend, the wise winter wanderer should have a companion or, better still, three. I recommend four as the ideal number for a winter trip. With three, one person always seems to get left out or left behind, and with two the margin of error, should things go wrong, is uncomfortably tight. For preference, then, make up a party of four; three if you cannot, two if you must, but except in well-travelled lowland areas think very hard indeed before going alone.

Quite apart from the safety angle, which tends to be over-laboured in outdoor books, there is the factor of companionship, but the most compelling reason is that a group can divide the necessary gear among the members and thus reduce each member's individual load. Weight is a real enemy out of doors. It slows you down, tires you out, and helps to produce perspiration.

Upgrading three-season equipment

The main items of equipment needed for comfortable travel and shelter in winter can all be upgraded to cope with fairly steep falls in temperature and the uncontrollable cold and damp.

Tents should have a flysheet and this should be pegged out close to the ground. Extra pegging loops sewn into the fly will help to ensure a close surface fit, and careful pitching, seeing that the inner tent is kept well away from the outer fly, will provide the necessary dead-air space needed for insulation. Double guying is essential in winter to cope with stronger winds and wind rock. A space blanket or bivvy bag spread *under* the groundsheet, or newspapers spread over the groundsheet inside the tent will increase ground insulation. Most insulation is lost through ground chill striking up from the snow or cold ground, and any spare insulation should go on the tent floor.

Sleeping-bag warmth can be improved by wearing loose wool pyjamas on top of thermal underwear, and by wearing socks and a hat. A hood added to the sleeping bag is also an aid to the occupants' warmth, but the greatest aid is adequate insulation from ground chill. A thin closed-cell ensolite sleeping pad is not adequate in winter, so use *two* such pads, or a thicker open-cell pad, or an air mattress. Remember to insulate the air mattress from the ground, and between mattress and sleeping bag, by using newspaper or spare clothing. Ground chill will otherwise chill the air in the mattress which in turn will chill anyone lying on it, for the air in the mattress is not dead but loose and able to circulate.

Stoves and cooking can be a problem in winter. All pots should have lids and the stove needs a windshield. If you are using gas as opposed to petrol, paraffin or solid fuel, it is necessary to keep the cartridges warm, as butane will not gasify below 0°C (32°F) and is a slow fuel close to zero anyway. It is better to invest in a petrol or paraffin stove. Matches are more effective than butane lighters for the same reason, but need to be shielded from damp in a sealed container.

During the day, items in the rucksack must be protected from rain, melting snow and, not infrequently, sweat. Few rucksacks are waterproof, so a large plastic dustbin liner can be fitted inside the sack to keep the rain off the contents. Even so, individual items, especially dry clothes and sleeping bags, should have their own nylon waterproof stuff-sack or plastic bag. Plastic bags, however mundane, are the secret weapon of the winter camper, and no one can have enough of them, plus plenty of thick elastic bands. I always carry a dozen or so looped round my ice axe or ski poles. Cold can make them brittle, but they don't get lost.

The best way to upgrade three-season equipment is by adding extra insulation, and remembering good technique. Stay dry and you will stay warm. Be active and you will stay warm. Choose careful pitches and use the wild to help you rather than fight it like an enemy. Three-season gear is really only adequate for low-level trips, if only because the extra gear necessary to upgrade it adds too much weight to the load, but for those initial trips, when you are learning about winter, such gear is usually adequate, and when you are acquiring technique will help to underline the fact that in winter good techniques are just as important (I nearly wrote *more* important) as the right equipment. In truth, you need both.

Tents

Tents for winter use come in various shapes and materials, but all have certain distinct and necessary features, notably the ability to shed wind and snow and provide adequate insulation. There are dome tents and mountain tents, tents in nylon and tents in Gore-Tex, but the standard winter tent is a steep-roofed ridge tent, with a ridge pole, and, for preference, A-poles as well.

Dome or pyramid tents, some in Gore-Tex, of wind-shedding geodesic design and resembling nylon igloos with hoops like the excellent ultimate Phazor Dome, are also coming on to the market. Though heavier and more expensive than ridge tents they are more

roomy and therefore attractive for small parties who can cram in
together and stay warm. The better ones can be pitched fly first, and
have good cooking and storage space. Mountain tents for use in
snow will have a tunnel on the fly to keep the snow out, and tents
can thereby be linked together. There are also the usual A-frame
ridge tents, following the most practical design for winter use, and
my personal choice.

As essential features the *winter* ridge tent must have a flysheet, a
good, deep tray-groundsheet, which is sometimes equipped with a
velcro or zip-shut cooking hole, and a wide skirt or snow-valance on

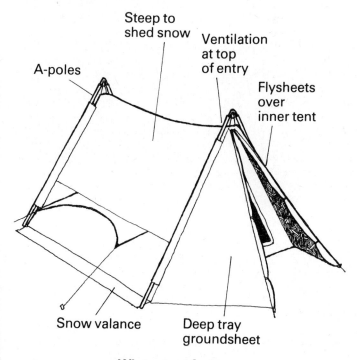

Winter tent features

the fly to help exclude the wind. It should pitch fairly low, shed wind, and steeply, to help shed snow. A ridge pole, to stress the fly, is helpful here, as are A-poles. Even specifically designed winter tents usually need some adaptation, notably the addition of extra guying points. The fly needs to have a good wide porch for storing gear and cooking. This, although risky, is often unavoidable in winter. Mountain tents with tunnel entrances do not always have this feature. A vital but often overlooked point is that *all* winter tents should provide adequate ventilation for the occupants. It may seem more cosy to exclude the cold night air, but ventilation is necessary to carry off cooking fumes, steam from pots, or human exhalations and moisture, all of which cause condensation. Beware of carbon monoxide and anoxia, and ventilate well. Some arctic tents tents are fitted with an extra interior flysheet called a 'frost liner', which is designed to trap and freeze such moisture under the fly and keep it from the tent walls. In practice I have found such liners more trouble than they are worth.

One final point is that a well designed winter tent should enable the occupant to pitch the fly first and strike it last, and so erect and strike the inner in shelter.

Winter tents tend to be heavier than similar summer models, and usually weigh in at around 4.5 kilos (10 lbs) or more. Winter tents are usually manufactured in rip-stop nylon. To work well in combating condensation, the inner tent must breathe, so only the groundsheet should be truly waterproof. The nylon flysheet, however, should be waterproof and this will inevitably trap and freeze warm air escaping from the inner tent. To maintain shape under stress, the ridge and main seams to guying points should be 'catenary' cut, which means they are cut on a bias which levels out when stressed and stops the panels wrinkling. Each person in the tent will exhale about one pint of water each night just in perspiration and breathing, and this causes condensation. Gore-Tex fabrics are being introduced into winter tents in an attempt to minimise condensation, but they are more expensive and not yet entirely effective. In winter, condensation in the tent is a fact of life,

Blacks Alaskan '80 mountain tent

but good ventilation and continual mopping can minimise it. Frozen condensation should be shaken off before the tent is packed away in the morning.

To sum up, then, the winter tent will be of snow- and wind-shedding configuration, and either ridge or dome-shaped. It will have a tray groundsheet, a fly with snow valance or skirt, facilities for sheltered storage and cooking, and points for extra guying. It may, according to design, have a tunnel entrance, a cooking hole, and perhaps a frost liner. It must be well manufactured, with catenary-cut seams on the fly which can be pitched first and struck last. The weight should be as little as possible, matched to strong manufacture.

Remember that the enemies to tent life in winter are wind and condensation. Other matters are debatable. Winter nights are long, and a cramped tent is a miserable place to spend perhaps fourteen hours of the day; on the other hand small tents are warmer. The buyer must consider all these points when buying a winter tent, and be prepared to add to and adapt the tent to suit his or her particular requirements. New designs are constantly coming on to the market and as good winter tents are expensive it would be advisable to study tent reports in the outdoor magazines before purchase. I should add that for the last three winters I have used a two-man nylon A-frame ridge tent, with pre-pitch fly, and found it quite adequate in snow at temperatures down to $-15°C$ (5°F), in mountains up to 3000 m. (9840 ft).

Pegs

The winter camper needs a variety of pegs to cope with ice, frozen ground, soft snow, or a mixture of all three. Extra guying points and double guying also require more pegs. The good old-fashioned wooden pegs are very useful in deep snow, but ice axes, skis or ski poles, crampons and 'deadmen' made from snow-filled stuff sacks may also be needed for main guys. Carry a variety of pegs and use every technique to ensure that when the tent goes up, it stays up. Pitching techniques are examined in Chapter 5.

Dome tent, winter in the Black Mountains

Poles

It is worth remembering that if the tent design calls for the poles to be planted in the ground, then on soft snow the poles will sink in as soon as stress is placed upon the guys. Some tents are designed with the poles fixed inside the groundsheet, or sleeved into the entrance corners, two features worth noting. Wise winter campers also carry a few flat discs (jam-jar lids are excellent) to place at the foot of the poles to provide extra support. Some poles are shock-corded and need only a shake to come together, a useful feature when anything which minimises the handling of cold metal objects is to be welcomed. In sub-zero conditions beware of handling metal objects with the bare hands, for the metal can freeze to your skin. Even thin gloves will give adequate protection.

Tent bags

Winter tents need to be kept in their bags or stuff-sacks. They will inevitably become wet, and need to be kept clear of the other items in the rucksack. If the opportunity occurs to stop in the sun and dry the tent out during the day, take it. A damp tent will gradually become uninhabitable in winter. Keep the fly and inner separate for the same reason, and fight damp all the time.

Sleeping bags

With sleeping bags we return to the issues covered when we considered anoraks, namely the choice of filling. The decision is simple. If you go camping in extreme conditions with reliable sub-zero weather, then down-filled bags, if properly constructed, are lighter and warmer. You also need good technique and constant vigilance to keep the inside of the tent and thus the bag dry.

Even in sub-zero temperatures, condensation in the tent or snow-hole can lead to dampness attacking the bag. If you are choosing a down bag for deep winter use, apart from good bag insulation, check the amount of actual down in the filling. Down consists of the soft under-feathers of geese and ducks. This is warm, soft and excellent, but often blended with larger feathers which are not so efficient. A 'down' bag, by BSI standards, must have 85% down. A 'down and feather' bag must have at least 51% down.

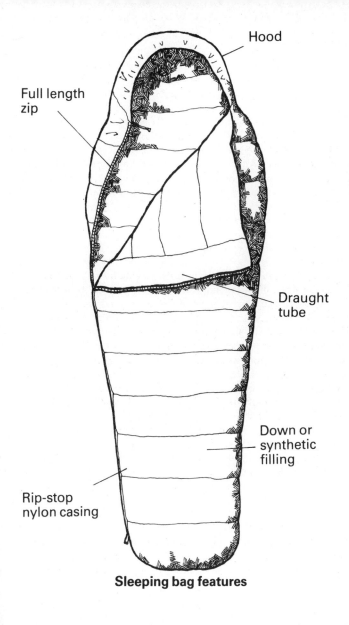

Hood

Full length
zip

Draught
tube

Down or
synthetic
filling

Rip-stop
nylon casing

Sleeping bag features

Don't buy a 'feather and down' bag, which needs to have only 15% down.

Since down loses its insulating properties when damp, people in more temperate climates, or those who camp below the snowline, should choose synthetic fillings, usually a Dacron derivative such as Fibrefill or Hollofil. Polarguard is a Celanese product, stiffer than the other synthetics but popular in the U.S.A. These fillings are warm even when damp, but are usually heavier, bulkier and difficult to pack. Bag shape is not critical and depends on the preference of the user. I feel trapped in a 'mummy' bag, but some people swear by them.

The real criterion of bag suitability, apart from the filling, is the construction, and a good winter bag must contain certain specific features. The winter camper looks for a bag which has a hood. The full-length zip must be flapped, and it should be possible to open the zip from the inside as well as the outside. One useful feature is a 'draught tube'. This is a long insulated tube running inside the zip which prevents the draught entering such an obvious cold spot. The bag should not be 'sewn-through', with inner stitched to outer, but have baffles to keep the filling well separated. Currently, the best method of bag construction has slant wall baffles, with differential cut, that is, the inner is smaller than the outer. This allows the filling to loft and the air spaces to multiply. Check the bag for good construction, for even distribution of the filling, and for neat stitches of not less than eight to the inch. Good bags have rip-stop nylon for the outer, but cotton (which is warmer) for the inside. Nylon interiors are chilly and clammy and need a cotton liner to make them really comfortable.

Catalogues describe bags in various ways, but a bag rated down to $-28.9°C$ ($-20°F$) should be adequate for most conditions. Weight of the filling is another useful guide, and a down bag should contain at least 1.5 kg (3 lb) of down. More synthetic filling is required to provide a similar amount of protection, so campers should look for weight in excess of 2.5 kg (5 lb) for a synthetic bag.

The features for your winter bag, then, are:

1. A hood.
2. A full-length zip with draught tube and interior pull.
3. Baffled, slant wall, differential-cut construction.
4. A minimum of 1.5 kg. (3 lb) of down or 2.5 kg (5 lb) of synthetic. More filling may be needed to cope with very cold conditions.
5. The casing should be rip-stop nylon and the inner of cotton. Always protect your bag in a nylon stuff-sack or a plastic bag, and when not in use take it out of the stuff-sack and hang it up loose. Prolonged compression results in a loss of loft.
6. Choose down for reliable sub-zero conditions and synthetics for less reliable conditions.

The secret of sleeping warm depends very much on technique. Get into dry clothes and into the bag while you are still warm from travel or setting up camp. Eat something to produce body heat. Wear a hat or socks, keep the shoulders covered, and a few minutes rapid isometric exercises, tensing and relaxing the muscles, can help the bag to warm up. If you get out at night, fold the top over to retain interior heat. When much of my down bag got wet last winter on a hut tour, I put on my dry clothes and slept *under it*, with the wet side on top, and had an adequate night's sleep. It may not work everywhere, and it is much better to keep the bag dry.

Mattress or air beds
I am very much addicted to a good night's sleep and, anyway, in a tent in winter there is not much else to do. I remember vividly one winter trip in the Cairngorms of Scotland when we went to bed on the mountain at 5.00 p.m. each night and stayed there, apart from periodic sorties, until 8.00 a.m. next day. You can catch up on a lot of sleep in the winter hills, if you can get to sleep in the first place.

Good insulation from ground chill is the secret of a good night's sleep. You will need something under your sleeping bag to provide this, the choice resting between the ensolite closed-cell pad, like the Karrimat, or the air-bed. Closed-cell pads do not provide adequate insulation, certainly not on snow, and are not all that comfortable. Open-cell pads, of 'egg-box' configuration, are much better but bulkier. Air beds are certainly comfortable but they are also heavy and bulky. Since the ground chills the free air inside they require double insulation, the bed from the ground *and* the sleeper from the bed. Short hip-length mattresses have been recommended and if you can work with them all well and good. I prefer a longer mattress.

A very useful compromise, and one which works, is in the recently introduced range of self-inflating mattresses, like the *Therm-a-rest* or the *Callipak*. These are of closed-cell construction, but when air is admitted through the valve they inflate to provide more insulation than an ensolite closed-cell pad, and as much comfort as an air bed. They can be easily deflated and, a great advantage, they roll up tightly. Various models are now on the market, and I would regard a self-inflating mattress as an essential winter purchase.

Stoves and fuel

Stoves and fuels have to be considered together in winter. Gas stoves are undoubtedly convenient, but gas is a troublesome fuel in winter, for the butane gas used in cartridges will not gasify at sub-zero temperatures. Gas-stove manufacturers are well aware of this and there are stoves on the market with pre-heat devices which warm the gas before it enters the burner. Some people recommend keeping gas cartridges inside the sleeping bag at night to keep them warm. Such techniques have their uses (and their problems) but for winter use it is as well to choose a stove which runs on a more practicable fuel. This means non-leaded petrol (white gas), paraffin (Kerosene), methylated spirits or solid fuel. I would not recommend solid fuel in winter, which leaves us with a choice between petrol, paraffin or meths, and the stoves which burn such fuels.

There are various petrol and paraffin stoves on the market, normally of the Primus-Optimus type. One recent innovation which has gained a great deal of popularity is the MSR Model G stove, which will burn a range of liquid fuels and works efficiently at all temperatures. This weighs 1.3 kg or 2 lb. 12oz. with a full Sigg bottle of fuel, and runs for one hour on one point of fuel. I personally use a petrol stove, the Optimum SVEA 123R, and find it very efficient. The SVEA is small, weighs 1 lb. 5oz. with a full tank, and will burn for over one hour on a single filling. It also has an integral windshield, and a metal cup as a protector. All petrol stoves have to be primed and the SVEA can be difficult to start. I use half a Meta solid fuel block to get it warm, and it then roars away merrily.

There are those who use, and swear by, the very popular Trangia stove, which runs on meths, has few movable parts and comes supplied with cookset and windshield. This is a good winter stove, but it does use a lot of fuel. I must recommend petrol or paraffin as the ideal winter fuel.

The winter camper should choose a stove which:

1. Runs on petrol, paraffin or meths.
2. Has a windshield.
3. Has a simmer control.
4. Contains fuel for at least one hour's cooking.
5. Is light in weight.

Stability is important in any stove, and it is a good idea, especially on snow, to support the stove with a fence of tent pegs. A small ensolite or asbestos pad under the stove is useful to prevent heat loss, aid starting, and stop a hot stove sinking out of sight. Take a small plastic funnel for refilling. A few spares like a pricker or fuel nipple should be taped to the stove. Spilling volatile fuel is inadvisable, so the stove should only be filled well away from the tent, using the funnel. A stove should NEVER be filled or, above all, LIT, inside a tent.

If you spill petrol on your hands in sub-zero conditions, the evaporation of the chill spirit will almost certainly cause rapid frostbite. Whenever I fill my SVEA in winter I use a funnel and hold the funnel with the pot-grab, just in case I spill the petrol out of the funnel.

Lighting a petrol stove in winter can be a problem. Most stoves require priming with meta-tablets or meths to get them warm and for the fuel to vapourise. Keep butane gas-lighters inside your clothing, to keep them warm, or they will not light either. On the other hand, matches kept inside clothing can become damp with sweat and need to be kept in the pack in a sealed container.

Cooksets

Metal cooksets are widely available and widely used, but remember that touching cold metal in winter can cost you the skin off your fingers, so where possible all items should be in plastic. Freeze-dried foods, which can be reconstituted with hot water while still in their plastic sleeves, save a lot of work.

I use and would recommend the Sigg range of pots, with a small Trangia kettle. The kettle, wrapped in a J-cloth to reduce rattling, sits inside the cookset. Mug and plate are plastic, as are the handles of my knife, fork and spoon, and the entire set has its own stuff-sack, to keep dirty pots away from other items in the sack. Plastic items can break very easily in sub-zero temperatures, but if metal items are used they must be taped here and there for ease of handling.

Water bottles

The winter walker and camper must drink a lot of water to avoid dehydration. Melting snow is not enjoyable and uses a lot of fuel, so it is usually necessary to transport water. A large one-litre metal or plastic bottle is ideal. Protect the bottle with a sock and, in very cold weather on the move, put the bottle inside the rucksack, close to your back, where body heat will keep it warm. A leather 'wine bag' held on a shoulder strap by dog lead clips, and kept inside the jacket, is another good idea. At night it is often necessary to take the bottle into your sleeping bag. Winter campers, according to some pundits, are apparently very keen on taking items into their sleeping bags. One author I read recently recommended taking into the sack your stove, boots, spare fuel cartridges, water bottle, wet clothing and large P-bottle. It must have got rather crowded. Water will freeze, though, and I find that the best place for the bottle is inside a sock and placed between the sleeping bags where movement and warmth will keep the water from freezing.

Smear Vaseline or some petroleum jelly around the screw-top to stop it freezing, and in very cold weather carry the bottle upside down so that, if ice does form, it will not congeal at the top and plug the aperture. It is worth restating that in dry, cold air the traveller dehydrates steadily. Drink often, using the warmer water in the bottle. Replenish the supply with cold water from a stream at every opportunity.

Pack frames or rucksacks

Looking around the winter world I think that the type of sack or pack-frame is unimportant. People use frames, or frameless rucksacks, internal frames or soft packs, and each seems happy with the choice. The important feature is that the sack should be big enough to hold all you need and no more.

Most outdoorsmen starting out on winter camping will already possess a rucksack. Lining it with a plastic bin liner and protecting the contents in plastic bags will help shield the contents from rain and melting snow, but to be efficient the winter sack does need some special features.

Ski-touring sacks will be discussed in a later chapter, but no winter sack for serious use is complete without both ice-axe loops and crampon straps. These items are essential for the winter hill walker, and the sack must be designed to carry them and have them readily to hand (or foot).

No nylon or canvas sack is truly waterproof. The better sacks, with the bottom sheathed in suède, or manufactured from Cordura fabric, are better than those in plain nylon, but all need assistance. Wrap the contents in stuff sacks, or use a plastic bin-liner. Zips should be of heavy duty plastic or metal, with long tabs, easy to pull shut or open while wearing gloves or mitts, or with chilled fingers. All zips should be flapped. Check that the zips close completely, otherwise snow and spindrift will infiltrate into the sack and wet the contents. Good sacks attempt to combat this with wide sealing tops and a waterproof baffle with a drawstring at the neck of the main compartment.

Most manufacturers of any repute make a range of good winter sacks, and Berghaus, Karrimor, Lowe Alpine, Camp Trails, Kelty, Bergen and Millet are just a few good makes. On sack capacity, one of 60 litres or a little more is about right. Winter gear is more bulky and frequently wet, so while the gear taken should always be the minimum consistent with comfort, a little extra space is often useful. A good comfortable hip harness and wide shoulder straps are

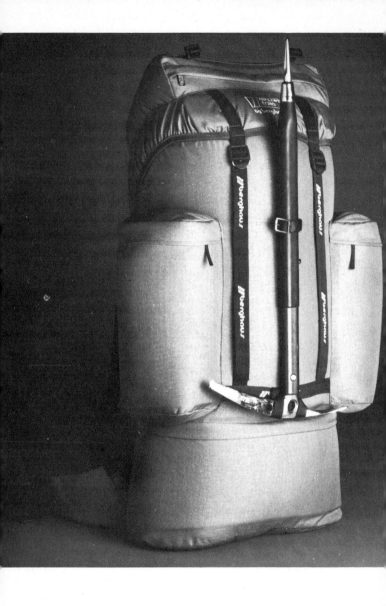

therefore useful. Cross-country sacks need a chest or 'sternum' strap as well.

Winter sack features are:

1. Water-resistant fabric and good construction.
2. Loops for the ice axe and crampon straps.
3. Flapped, fully closing zips.
4. An interior main compartment baffle.
5. Adequate capacity of 60 litres or more.
6. Comfortable shoulder straps and hip harness.

Lights

It is often useful to have the hands free and for this reason I use a belt-pack torch with an optional headlamp. The headlamp can be directed into whatever task is in hand from stirring the stew to reading, while the torch itself, complete with battery, is clipped inside my shirt pocket and kept warm. Always carry spare bulbs and batteries among the group.

For longer-term illumination, especially in a snow-hole, a candle is sufficient, and wide-based long-life candles are better then the slender household types. In fact I use communion candles, the thick type sold for churches. I chop off a length as I need it and they last for ages. Any naked flame in a tent must be deplored, but if you keep the candle inside the lid of your cookset it will be quite safe. Trim the wick to avoid smoke sooting up the roof. This will also produce a useful amount of warmth, but it can also produce condensation and reduce the oxygen content. A little ventilation is required. A candle really comes into its own in a snow-hole where the light reflecting from the crystals provides plenty of illumination. Candle lanterns are popular but not strictly necessary, while some people go the whole hog and carry paraffin or gas storm lanterns. It's all weight, but if you are prepared to hump them, it's up to you.

Berghaus Cyclops Echo rucksack

Heat
There are small heaters on the market, but I can't think of anywhere I would use one. Use dry clothing, a decent bag, a square meal, and good technique, and produce your own warmth internally.

Radio
I have recently acquired a small compact transistor radio, ostensibly for hearing weather forecasts, actually to while away the nights. Reception in the hills is fitful, but I enjoy it and have been able to pick up forecasts and avalanche warnings. Purists can use an earpiece to save annoying the other people in the tent or hut. This is really an optional item, but I find it useful.

P-bottle
One of the disadvantages of long nights in a tent or snowhole, especially if the occupants spend the dark hours swilling tea or spirituous liquor, is that sometime in the wee chill dark hours nature will come hammering on the door. I don't know what to do about this, except get up and get it over with as quickly as possible. Lying there, losing sleep and wondering if you can hang on till dawn, seems the worst of all worlds. One much-touted masculine solution, which I offer for what it's worth, is to carry a large, wide-necked bottle and use that. Those who use them, swear by them. The only other advice in this connection is to beg you never to melt yellow snow!

Compass and maps
A compass, large-scale maps and a constant use of both is always advisable and sometimes essential in winter. Plan the route carefully before leaving base and use the evenings to study maps of the next day's route and prepare a route card. Trying to open out a map and plot a bearing out on the hill in wind-blown snow is next to impossible. Copying the grid numbers into the 10 km squares saves opening the map for references. Protect the maps in a plastic bag or map case, and if you have time to proof the maps with some plastic screen, so much the better.

Wear the compass around your neck, but tucked away where it

cannot fly up into your face. I have a nice new scar on my forehead received from the edge of my compass, following a fall on a ski-tour in Colorado.

Navigation can be difficult in winter, and skill with map and compass is a prerequisite for successful trips. Winter restricts visibility, woods lose their shape and hills become identical. Maps of 1:25000 scale are most useful in winter, but those used to the more popular 1:50000, or the 1 inch to 1 mile series, may take some time to get used to the different scales and distances involved. Beware of losing height when contouring in poor weather.

First-aid kit
A few items should be added to the usual summer kit of plasters, bandages and Savlon cream. A good lip salve and a barrier cream for the face and hands should be carried and repeatedly applied, especially after washing or drinking. Chapped face and hands or cracked lips may not be very dangerous but they are not much fun either and can easily be avoided. A full first-aid kit should be carried as a group item. First-aid treatment in winter will be covered in a later chapter.

Survival kit
To some degree all the equipment and clothing carried or worn in winter is survival equipment, and I would again wish to discourage the notion that anyone entering the winter hills is, by that very action, putting him- or herself in a survival situation. If you have the ability to use the following, and the sense to carry them, a survival situation will either not arise or be containable. These items are popularly referred to as the Ten Essentials:

1. Map and compass
2. Whistle
3. 'Bivvy' bag
4. Candle
5. Spare food (chocolate)
6. Spare sweater
7. Matches or lighters
8. First-aid kit
9. Sleeping bag
10. Torch

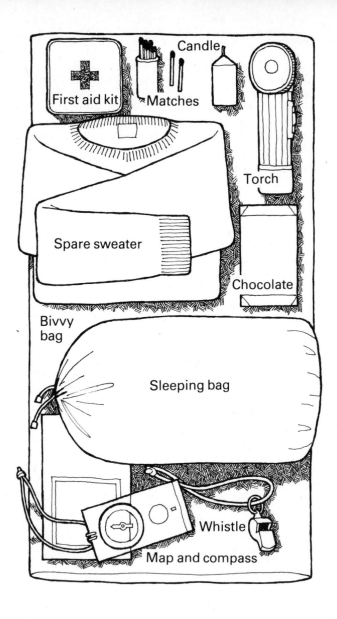

A few flares and smoke cannisters and a shovel blade that fits to an ice-axe can be carried as group items. Most of this kit the winter outdoorsman will be carrying anyway; but the items are listed because, even on a day or half-day tour or hill walk, it would be very sensible if everyone carried these items in a small rucksack, and *essential* that a group carries them. Remember that the usual yellow bivvy bag shows up well against the snow, a good marker for rescue teams or helicopters.

You may, and indeed probably will, carry these items for years without any need to use them, but they weigh very little and indicate a sensible level of caution. Then, when (not if) something does go wrong, you will be well equipped to survive.

Repair kit
In summer, if something goes wrong with the gear, you just curse and press on. In winter this may be inadvisable or impossible. A jammed zip may make a tent unusable, a snagged bag may leak all its filling. The group should carry a repair kit including some safety pins, nylon line and a needle and thread, some twine and rip-stop tape. It can also be useful for the repair of clothing.

Flasks
One very useful item in winter is the vacuum flask. This can contain hot tea, soup or a fairly liquid stew, which will provide a quick, nourishing and warm midday meal. I must confess that my own experience with vacuum flasks has been mixed, mainly because when I come to use them I find that the interior contains a mass of broken glass. However, if you have one, and can protect it, they can be very useful. I do have and use a hip-flask, which is regularly charged with the finest products of Speyside. To take alcohol or not is a personal choice and I never carry enough to force it on others. It adds nothing to body warmth, but a nip before sleep is a pleasant custom.

Sundry items
Weight inside the average rucksack is largely caused by the inclusion of little items taken 'because they weigh nothing'.

Everything weighs something – don't kid yourself. The less taken the better, but the following may prove useful.

Plastic bags are a real boon, and have a lot of uses. They can hold wet clothes, act as overshoes if all else fails, and keep the clothing dry. Stuff-sacks are essential for keeping the snow and spindrift out of spare clothing and sleeping bag.

Keeping the tent dry largely means keeping the snow out, and some people carry a small stiff brush to dust the snow from boots and clothing and several porous J-cloths to mop up moisture from the groundsheet. A switch cut from a small fir can serve as a brush, but a few mopping cloths are useful.

Toilet paper is obvious, but take a few small packets of paper tissues too. Winter being what it is, the nose runs all the time and handerkerchiefs are unhygienic, quickly get wet, and make the nose sore. Nose-blowing with the fingers is a technique worth practicing.

Spare line is needed for double-guying the tent, or in extreme cases for preparing a stretcher or a shelter. About 15 metres should be sufficient and your avalanch cord can always be used for this purpose.

Selection of gear

After these two chapters the reader may be appalled at the amount of gear required, and the weight he apparently has to carry. I agree that it does concentrate the mind. When going on a winter trip, some method should be found for eliminating excess weight and avoiding the duplication of items. The best way to do this is in the pre-trip planning stage, when an accurate equipment list should be prepared by the leader and then studied and criticised by at least one other member of the party. Take all that you *need*, some things that you want, but nothing that you just *fancy*.

Once the *total* amount of equipment is agreed, group items should be marked, as here, with a 'g', and divided, by weight, among the members of the party. Such action, apart from sharing the load, does provide a powerful incentive for the group to stay together and act as a team, or at least as a group of mutually dependent friends.

A full list of clothing and equipment is given in Appendix 1, but this list will illustrate the point.

Kit lists

Tent (g)	Rucksacks
Poles (g)	Compass
Pegs (g)	Maps
Sleeping Bags	Survival Kit (g) - ?
Sleeping Mats	First-aid Kit (g) - ?
Stove (g)	Water Bottles
Cookset (g)	Torch
Plates	Candles (g)
Mugs	Flasks (g)
Cutlery	Plastic Bags (g)

As you can see, a surprising number of items can be carried on a group basis, like the tent, where inner, fly, poles and pegs can be shared, or the stove, where only one is really required. Take the lightest, most efficient items that the group happens to possess, and pare away relentlessly at weight. People may well argue with this in detail, and indeed, I would lean towards the idea that everyone should take their own compass and survival kit, although they could well be group items. It is a very good idea to weigh each item and note the weights on the kit list.

No one will dispute that weight in winter is a significant factor and all steps must be taken to reduce it to the minimum, particularly when touring on skis. I have toured with 7.5 kilos (16 lb) and 23 kilos (50 lb) and the lower the better, believe me.

One other way to concentrate the minds on this issue is to have a kit meeting. Let *all* the kit, including personal items, be brought to a meeting and piled in the middle of the floor. Even for a weekend trip this is a daunting sight. Then let each member select and take back his own items, while the rest offer comments on what is needed or not. This should reduce the amount of personal extras, which is a group factor. People may say that if they are prepared to carry it, it's up to them, but in winter this is only true within limits. The group must stay together and not have to cope with an overburdened member. Don't forget that the weight of food, fuel and water must be added to the basic kit load.

Once personal gear has been minimised the 'group' items should

be distributed and checked against the previously prepared master list (See Appendix 1). Don't take anything unnecessary, but don't leave anything vital behind. Check gear into the rucksacks, and into the transport and out again, noting who has what. With any luck you will have everything you need and nothing to spare.

Snow camping with a ridge tent

'Tis a gross error to believe that fortune always favours fools'

John Gay

It is perfectly possible to walk and camp for years in winter without ever entering into the hills or setting foot on snow. Possible perhaps, but not much fun. The walker who stays low down in winter will be missing a great deal and not taking full advantage of winter's many opportunities.

To enter the winter hills and travel safely, though, the traveller needs to acquire a few items of equipment and learn to use them. These are:

1. An ice axe.
2. Crampons.
3. A snow shovel.

Various types of each item are available, together with a number of useful accessories.

Unless on skis or snow-shoes, most winter travellers will wear the usual vibram cleated-sole boots. In winter the boots should be heavier and stiffer, but the fact remains that when crossing icy rocks or snow crust, the rubber sole on its own is simply not adequate. Rubber cleated soles give insufficient grip, and if the route is exposed rubber-soled boots may be lethal. These soles grip well on dry rock, but in winter the rock is rarely dry, while the lug-spaces of the sole clog up with snow or mud, and become smooth and slippery. It is a fact that the major cause of hill accidents is slips, and the major cause of slips is worn or unsuitable footwear.

The answer in such circumstances is the wearing of crampons and the use of an ice axe, both of which are essential items of winter equipment.

Ice axes

Any walker entering the hills in winter must carry an ice axe, and carry it in his or her hand, ready for use, not strapped to the rucksack as a good-luck charm. The ice axe is designed to be used and has a wide application. With an ice axe the walker can gain precious support in tricky sections, and cut steps in frozen snow or ice when it is too hard for step-kicking with the boots. It can be used to probe the depth of snow; as a firm, deep tent-peg; to test the thickness of ice on frozen streams and, above all, as a brake for self-arrest in the event of a slip.

The walker will usually encounter snow and ice somewhere in winter on any hill over 500 m. (1500 ft). Mountains over 2000 m. (7000 ft) often have snow cover all the year round, especially in gullies or on sheltered north-facing slopes. An ice axe is by no means only a winter tool, and the criterion is that it should be carried wherever and whenever it might prove useful, not just in the obvious winter season.

Like all tools it takes time and practice to become experienced with an ice axe, and even the experienced walker will need to take a little time each winter to re-learn the skills of self-arrest and step-cutting before entering the hills for a trip.

Choosing an ice axe

There is a wide variety of ice axes on the market, but not all of them are suitable for walkers and backpackers. Climbers' ice axes tend to be too short. As a guide, the spike of the walker's ice axe should just clear the ground when held at your side, by the head, with the arm slightly bent. Ice-axe shafts come in glass fibre, metal, or various woods – ash, hickory or bamboo – or a laminate. The shaft should be oval in section rather than round, as this gives a better grip. The steel head should have a long, only slightly curved pick, with a serrated inner edge, while the adze-head should be curved rather than straight to help clear the chips away when step-cutting on ice.

Walkers, if offered the choice, should buy an axe with 'positive' pick clearance, in which the bottom of the pick slants down to the rear serrated edge. This is more suitable for step-cutting and self-arrest on ice than the upward-slanting 'negative' pick clearance.

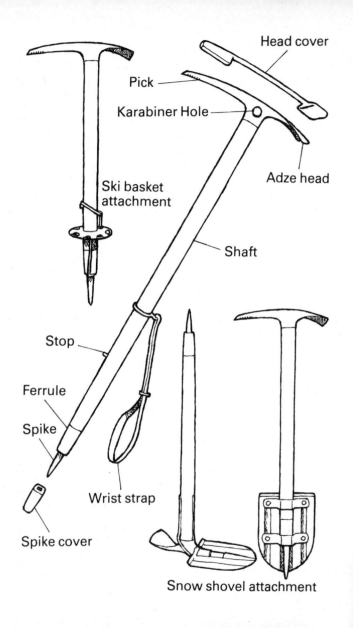

Head cover

Pick

Karabiner Hole

Adze head

Ski basket attachment

Shaft

Stop

Ferrule

Spike

Wrist strap

Spike cover

Snow shovel attachment

Good axes conform to UIAA standards. Most axes come equipped with a Karabiner hole in the head, and sometimes with a 'glide ring'. A leather or canvas wrist strap can be attached to the glide ring, which slides along the shaft. Opinions vary as to whether ice axes should be equipped with a wrist strap or loop. One opinion says that they should, so that in the event of a fall the axe stays with the walker for use in self-arrest or to climb up again after the fall. Others say that such loops are unnecessary or even dangerous, since in the event of a slip the walker will cling to the axe shaft anyway. If he does not, having a loose axe flailing about on the end of the sling is an added hazard. Personally, I lean towards the former school, since the danger of losing the ice axe outweighs the possibility of any accidental damage. If the axe is not equipped with a glide ring and strap, one can be fitted, or a nylon sling can be attached to the axe through the Karabiner hole in the head. The axe needs a double loop in the sling so that the short loop is employed when holding the axe by the head, and the long loop when the axe is being held at the spike end for step-cutting.

To gain a more secure grip on the handle and also, with metal and plastic shafts, for additional warmth, wrap the handle's mid-section with insulating tape, coiling it down from the head in overlapping loops. Cross-country ski waxes can also be rubbed on the shaft to improve grip. Metal axe-heads get very cold in winter, so that a little tape around the head-shaft at the point where the head is held can be useful in keeping the fingers warm.

It is possible to rent ice axes, but if so the complete axe and wrist loops should be carefully examined for wear, dents and hairline cracks. All regular winter travellers should have their own axe.

Accessories
The ice axe as described and illustrated so far is a basic winter tool, but various accessories exist which can widen its uses in deep snow.

In soft snow an ice axe is not much use as a means of support or indeed as an aid to balance, since it offers no resistance to the snow, and sinks straight in. A ski-basket fitted to the spike, lashed into place or held firm with a jubilee clip, can turn the axe into a miniature ski-stick and offer useful support. M.S.R. (Mountain

Safety Research) also produces a clamp-on snow-shovel blade which converts the axe into a shovel ideal for snow-holing.

Two essential extras for use when transporting the axe are a rubber or leather headguard, and a rubber spike-guard, which will stop the sharp edges digging holes in car seats or one's companion's anatomy. Some airlines refuse to carry axes without such protection, even in the luggage hold, and ice axes are not permitted in the passenger cabin. Spike-guards are very losable items, so it is best to have two.

Carrying the ice axe
My ice axe gets strapped to the pack in early October, when I am getting my basic winter kit assembled and checked over. There it stays until well into spring, unless I am on a lowland ramble, or it is actually in my hand, in use.

All good winter rucksacks must have an ice-axe loop at the bottom and straps centrally on the outer shell. Strap the axe on securely, and plug the protruding spike. Short climbing axes may fit within the overall length of the sack, but most walking axes protrude and need protecting. When travelling it is not a bad idea to put the axe inside the sack where it is protected against damage and theft. Head- and spike-guards can freeze to the metal in winter, so it is as well to remove them before leaving lower ground. At this stage the axe can be carried in the straps or tucked down between the rucksack and your back. This is uncomfortable, but it leaves the hands free.

Once on snow or icy paths, however, the ice axe *must be in your hand*. Have a rule about this, because it is very easy to plod on ever higher, thinking that you will stop in a minute to get the axes out, until someone falls and skids aways – at which point everyone hurriedly deploys their ice axes . . .

Carrying the ice axe in your hand is a matter fraught with controversy, and two schools debate which way you should carry the sharp pick. One school says keep the sharp bits, spike and pick, in view, and therefore pointing forward. Certainly if the axe is being

Winter walker in the Picos de Europa

carried by the centre of the shaft, the spike must point forward. There is, however, another school of thought which says that the axe, which is always held in the uphill hand, is carried pick to the rear, so that in the event of a slip, the shaft can be slapped up into the downhill hand and the axe-head is ready, pick down, for self-arrest. I have consulted various authorities on this point and, more usefully, consulted many photographs of experienced people using ice axes, and the numbers carrying them pick forward or backward seem to be equally divided. I would opt myself for the pick-to-the-rear position.

As soon as the slope gets steep, and unless the axe is in use for step-cutting, the walker should carry the axe in the 'ready' position, ready for self-arrest in the event of a slip.

The shaft is across the body, the spike towards or even into the slope for balance, the head held at shoulder height, the pick held downwards or to the rear. This is the 'ready' position for a *shoulder brake*, the basic self-arrest position.

Self-arrest

The first point to make is that self-arrest is not easy. It is a skill, and one which takes practice, nerve and strength. A slip on a steep slope is frightening, but you must keep your head. Wearing windproofs or non-'anti-glis' clothing will cause you to pick up speed very quickly and you must act fast.

To practise this skill, find a steep but short slope with a good, safe, rock-free run-out at the bottom. Wear gloves, cagoule and overtrousers. These will keep you dry and, since they are slippery, they will give you a little speed. It is hard to learn this skill usefully without moving. If climbing helmets are available, then wear one. You must be able to self-arrest from any position, but we will start with a simple slip.

Feet first

Assume the 'shoulder brake' position and when high and clear on the slope, fall on to your front and induce a slide. It is not a bad idea, on your safe practice slope, to have a few slides on your back and front before attempting to brake, just to see what happens. In

Arresting falls

Feet first

Assume shoulder brake position, fall on front and induce a slide.

Hold ice axe firmly across chest. Press pick in and arrest fall.

Head first

Plant pick in snow and swivel into the position shown above.

windproofs you will pick up speed very quickly, so the first rule is to brake fast *before* you pick up too much speed.

Hold the axe firmly across the chest, keep the hands low, and press the pick firmly but SLOWLY into the snow crust or ice using the shoulder. The shaft and spike end should project beyond the other arm. Let your body-weight rest on the axe and *keep your hands low*. The weight of your body will press the pick in and arrest your fall.

Needless to say, it is not as easy as that, but at least avoid these mistakes:

1. Do not try and slam the pick into the ice. It will bounce out again.
2. Do not let the axe get beyond the shoulder level or at arm's length. If you do, then, when you brake, the weight of your sliding body will tear the axe from your grasp and you will slide on with the axe flailing about your head, at the end of the sling.
3. Don't let go of the axe.

If you are wearing crampons keep the feet clear of the snow.

If you fall on to your back or side the same rules apply. Roll over, pressing the pick in slowly, use body-weight, and act fast but calmly. Practise, practise, practise. Once this has become fun, at least on the practice slope, make it more difficult.

Head first
If the slip is sudden and you fall awkwardly you may be sliding in a head-first fall position before you realise it. Before attempting self-arrest you must turn into the feet-first position.

To do this, use the pick. Plant it firmly but calmly into the snow at the waist-to-hip level, at mid-point of the body. You will then swivel round, and it is most important (and difficult) to keep the hands low and the body over the shaft as you spin around the embedded pick. You may need to roll over off your back, but the basics, which you must cling to, are:

1. Hands low.
2. Press the pick in slowly, using the shoulder.

Once you have got the hang of these arrests, try sliding down in the sitting position and rolling over into the arrest, or taking a dive off the top, with and without the rucksack. All this only on the safe practice slope – nowhere else.

Learning self-arrest is best handled as a game, but at the back of your mind remember that it is *not* a game, but an essential outdoor skill. Most hill-walking accidents are caused by slips. To avoid becoming a statistic, learn and practise self-arrest. Make a point of practising self-arrest quite often, and from a number of positions.

Two final points. If you are not wearing crampons the feet can be forced into the crust to help you stop. However, if you *are* wearing crampons the first thought when you slip must be to lift the feet high. If the crampon spikes catch you will go cartwheeling down the hill and all hope of stopping is gone, and the best you can hope for is torn ligaments in the ankle.

The point I must stress is PRACTICE. Crossing a steep, exposed slope on ice or crusty snow is a 'gripping' experience, even if heights don't bother you. If you slip, the hours spent practising will be vital to your well-being, even if, in the panic of the moment, you only remember the basics but somehow manage to stop. There is not much glamour in self-arrest, and a slip is something to avoid at all costs. Pick your route carefully and check around to see where you will end up if you slip. *That* should make you careful.

Step-kicking
Walking in snow, even if it is only ankle-deep, is slow and tiring, while anything much deeper than this puts long trips completely out of the question unless the traveller is wearing snow-shoes or cross-country skis, or following a well-trodden trail.

When travelling on snow, the walker learns to get up early and be on the move while the crust is still frozen and able to offer adequate support. Once the sun gets up and softens the crust, walking becomes a real chore, even on the flat, while whatever the snow state, it takes technique to climb and descend steep snow slopes.

Few things are more disconcerting than an insecure foothold, and the first technique the winter walker should learn on snow or ice is to plant the foot firmly, stamping the boot-sole firmly down and into

Kicking steps downhill. Keep weight forwards.

Kicking steps uphill. Kick through crust and test each step.

Cutting steps uphill. Stand upright and use adze part of axe, use inner hand for balance.

the surface, rather than placing it gingerly on top. This gives the boot a better grip even on crust, ice or *verglas*. Winter boots should be heavier and stiffer soled than summer footwear, which makes them more suitable for the hard work of kicking steps in snow crust and for wearing crampons.

When ascending a slope the natural tendency is to lean inwards, away from the drop. Resist this and stay vertical, planting the ice axe firmly, holding it in the uphill hand, and kicking through the crust into the snow. Use a direct forward swinging motion of the foot and kick straight ahead or even a little downwards to provide a firm platform for the foot. Test the foothold by putting a little weight on it. On a traverse, use the uphill edge of the boot as a cutting edge, rather than hammering ahead with the toe.

A flat or inward-sloping foothold is important, for the leader's footholds will be used by those behind and, if the foothold slopes back, someone will slip as the hold becomes firmly packed and icy. Keep the steps small, and if the slope is steep or very long traverse it in a series of diagonals. If the slope is short and steep you can scale it directly, holding the axehead in both hands, and planting it straight in front of you to help you up the slope. Kicking steps is hard work, so the leadership of the line should change periodically.

If the snow is too hard for kicking steps then the ice axe can be employed to cut them or you can put on the crampons.

Cutting steps

Crossing a slope, hold the axe at the spike end and, keeping it to the wrist with the long loop, cut a slash in the crust ahead with an even swing of the adze. There is really no need for much effort; the weight of the axe alone should be sufficient to carve out a platform wide enough to take the boot. Try and slant the cut into the crust. Balance upright on both feet and stand still when step-cutting, aiming for a full arm swing. You can use either arm, whichever seems most natural, although the outer one seems easier to me and leaves the inner hand free for balance. Step-cutting, like self-arrest, takes practice.

Whenever possible, the hill walker and backpacker should stay off ice. Certainly ice climbing as such, is outside the scope of this book. Winter being what it is, walkers will often encounter ice, frequently under a thin layer of snow, and to cross safely requires a knowledge of the ice-axe and crampon technique, even if the walker has every intention of staying on safe ground.

Step-cutting on ice is easier with the pick. Start the cut with that, and widen the step with the adze. When not wearing crampons, cut a step wide enough for the complete boot-sole and slant it inwards. An outward-slanting step would be dangerous. If the ice is firm or the snow a little crusty, a step wide enough for half the boot should give sufficient support and save a lot of work.

Step-kicking and cutting need to be practised on safe, but not simple, slopes. It may seem straightforward there, but on a steep exposed slope with black rocks jutting through the snow far below, it will be a different matter. Take your time, keep your nerve, and all will be well.

Descending

Any walker knows that coming down a hill can be even more tiring than climbing up. The same is true in snow. Coming down a snow slope or gulley can be even more unnerving than climbing up, or on a traverse. To avert the gaze from the drop, there is a natural tendency to descend the slope in a series of short shuffles or side-steps, using the edges of the boots. On all but very steep, practically concave snow slopes, it is far better to come down facing directly down the slope, planting the boot heel firmly in the snow and using your weight for grip and to penetrate the crust. Bend the knees and keep the weight forward. If you lean back on stiff legs, your boots will slip from under you and a slide is inevitable. A straight descent in this manner is the same under most conditions, but it takes some getting used to every winter.

Forced off the Canigou ridge in the Pyrenees, it took us an hour or two to get used to plunging down snow gullies, but confidence grows with practice and by the afternoon we were coming straight down almost vertical gullies, up to our thighs in snow at every step, but feeling – and being – very safe. Snow gullies should normally be avoided as they are often avalanche chutes, but needs must . . .

Having said that, beware; there are snags. If the snow is firmly iced over, the grip may be insufficient. If the snow is soft and deep, you may go in too deep at speed, and wrench a knee. Hidden rocks may trap an ankle.

The general rule, though, for plunge-stepping is to face down the slope and get as much of the boot sole on or in the snow as possible.

If the snow is too hard to give a safe grip you must kick-step. Plant the axe for support, and kick a step out below you with your heel. If the slope is too steep for this, plant the axe, face inwards, and, holding the axe head with both hands, kick steps down with the toe. If the snow is too hard for this, or ice appears, cut out steps with the axe, always making a firm, wide platform when descending, for the grip is always less secure. Better still, find another way. You have a problem.

Glissading

Glissading, quite simply, is sliding down a snow slope on the soles of your boots. I hesitated before including glissading in this book because it is undoubtedly dangerous and therefore a practice to be deplored. However, you may wish to make a voluntary glissade, so it would be as well to do it properly. If you are doing it deliberately, then there are rules. Don't try glissading unless you know the slope. One rule of thumb has it that you should never glissade down a slope you have not previously climbed. On the other hand, if the slope is safe, you can save time and enjoy an effortless descent.

The sitting glissade can be fun on safe slopes, if you are wearing windproof trousers. Sit down, raise the feet and set off, holding the axe spike on one side to act as a brake. To stop, dig in the heels, dig in the axe or, if going uncomfortably fast, roll over into self-arrest.

The standing glissade is more *macho*. Point the feet down the slope, keeping them well apart, with one foot slightly ahead. Bend the knees, and rest the ice-axe spike in the snow. You can (perhaps) slow your progress by digging the spike deeper, while to go faster you bring the feet closer together and stand more erect.

To stop, dig in the heels and ice axe, or turn the feet out, as for a stem ski-turn. Glissading is not a serious technique and has inherent dangers, but if you have a safe slope and a spare half-hour it's fun to try.

Crampons

The second major tool of the winter traveller is the crampon. Crampons are spiked strap-on boot-soles which give grip on ice or packed snow.

Wearing crampons is a major contribution to safety in the mountains for, it must be said again, lug-soles on their own are insufficient on wet, icy, or snow-packed slopes.

Crampon selection

There are various types of crampons, and each has its purpose. Casual walkers in Austria often use heel-crampons, a spiked metal boot-rim which is strapped over the boot-heels to give just a little extra grip on shallow slopes or in icy streets.

Instep crampons are for the more serious walker and can provide adequate protection on quite steep slopes. They can also be used with certain types of skis (Harscheisen) and are frequently used for winter hill-walking.

The two main types are the full sole 10- or 12-point crampons. Climbers opt for the 12-point, the two extra points being 'lobster claw' points which project from the front of the crampons and are used in ice-climbing when front-pointing, a technique which is outside the scope of this book. With 10-point crampons, which are sometimes called *walker's crampons*, the second set of points are omitted and the lobster claws are bent vertically downwards, to give a toe grip for climbing or descending modest slopes. There is some debate on the need for more than 10 points. My personal feeling is that while 10 points are quite adequate for all the activities within the scope of this book, using 12-point crampons is no great drawback. I use 12-point or 10-point, whichever come to hand, without worrying about it.

Buying and fitting crampons

Crampons have to be fitted to the boots, and the fit must be firm and accurate. This means that the boot-sole must be fairly rigid. Most popular makes, like the Salewa, come dismantled, and while it is possible to assemble the crampons and crampon straps yourself, my advice is to take your boots to the shop and have an experienced member of the staff fit them up.

Crampons come in two main sections, heel and sole, connected by a hinged metal 'joining bar'. This bar allows the boot to flex somewhat, and enables the fitter to adapt the crampon for length. Very flexible boots are not suitable for use with crampons.

When correctly fitted, the front lobster claws on 12-point

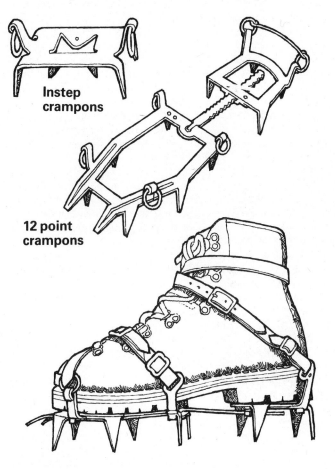

Instep crampons

12 point crampons

crampons protrude about 25 mm. (1 in.) beyond the boot. On
10-point models, the front down-point should be flush with the edge
of the sole at the toe. A metal strap or 'back-bar' is supplied for the
heel and this is pulled up over the heel welt. With this in place and
the boot firmly in the crampon it should be possible to pick up the
unstrapped boot and shake it without the crampon falling off. It is
essential to examine the fit from all angles, and see that the
crampon fits the boot-sole closely at all points. Crampon straps
should be of neoprene, for canvas straps freeze and are stiff to
handle.

To put the crampons on, spread out the straps, and plant the boot
firmly in the crampon, pulling up the back bar. Now shake the foot
again lightly. If the crampon stays firm, strap up the crampon firmly
but not tightly. Any compression on the foot, reducing circulation,
is an aid to frostbite and crampons themselves are a chilling agent,
drawing heat from the foot.

Carrying crampons
Spiked metal feet are awkward items to transport. Most good winter
rucksacks will have crampon straps and a reinforced patch to
contain them, either on the front or on the top flap. One essential
extra is a pair of rubber crampon-protectors, which cover the spikes
when the crampons are on the sack. Crampons can also be rolled up
in a cloth and carried inside the rucksack.

Walking in crampons
Walking in crampons takes practice. They should always be worn
with gaiters to avoid a spike catching in a flapping trouser leg, and
even with gaiters all laces and straps should be firmly tucked away.

Crampons will give a good grip on ice and hard-packed snow, and
once you get used to the 'up in the air' feeling, they feel very secure.
The rules for walking in crampons are simple. Walk slowly, plant
your feet firmly and use as many points as possible. Even two points
will often be adequate, but the more the better. Flex your ankles
freely to ensure this, an action which, as you will soon realise, is very
tiring.

Traversing on ice or crust it is possible to point the downhill foot

directly down the slope, so that all the points on that foot grip, while
moving the upper foot forward. This is tiring but useful for crossing
steep narrow snow gullies. On anything wide, or for ascending, the
walker should traverse. Exaggerate the movement, stepping wide to
keep the points from snagging, and plant the crampon firmly so that
it bites firmly into the crust. When descending steep slopes, walk
straight down, using the axe as a rail, planting it ahead and sliding
your hand down it as you descend.

In soft snow the crampons will ball up and this snow needs to be
knocked free of the spikes with a tap from the ice axe. Do this
frequently for balled-up crampons are dangerous on frozen crust.

Care of crampons
Crampons can easily become blunted on rock and need to be
sharpened from time to time. Metal fatigue is also a consideration,
particularly if they are worn with flexible-soled boots. Check the
screws and studs. Check the straps for wear and replace if necessary.

Finally, before leaving this section, a few points should be
stressed and remembered. The winter traveller needs an ice axe and
crampons, and the ability to use them, for safe walking in winter.
They are not discussed here as an aid to ice-climbing or as an excuse
for taking foolish risks. If you would not attempt something in
summer without crampons or ice axe, do not attempt it in winter
when wearing them. The line between climbing and hill walking is
often a fine one and the simplest break point is to say that you are
climbing when you have to use your hands and wish you had a rope.

On the other hand, it is pointless to pretend that difficult
situations can always be avoided. In the winter hills the traveller will
encounter clear grass, soft snow and crust, icy rocks, exposed slopes
of frozen snow, icy gullies, and much more. All must be anticipated
and none is insuperable, given good equipment, technique and,
eventually, experience. If you still find something you don't fancy or
can't handle, then common sense should point to the correct course
– retreat.

Walking-sticks
One useful and quite untechnical winter tool is the simple walking

stick. For probing snow, for testing ice, for extra support or balance, a walking-stick can come in very handy.

Snow shovels

I am a firm advocate of the snow shovel as a winter tool. They are not particularly awkward or heavy and have a multitude of uses. They can dig a snow-hole, erect a wall, dig a latrine, support the stove, act as a heat and light reflector, and do duty as a 'deadman' or a tent peg.

It is possible to buy just the blade which clamps to the ice-axe shaft, or buy a proper folding shovel. Eastern Mountain Sports have one which is 32.59 cm. (13 in.) and weighs only 198 gm. (6.5 oz.). The *Witco* snow shovel from Norway is only 35.13 cm. (14 in.) long and weighs 560 gm. (23 oz.). A snow shovel can always be carried as a group item, and will be found most useful for snow-holing, digging out a tent, or making a windbreak. Never use your snow shovel on a main guy. It may give good support, but you will probably need the shovel for digging.

Practice

One word, *practice*, appears again and again in this chapter. Mastery of ice axe and crampons is essential for the winter walker, and such mastery can only be acquired and maintained with practice.

Witco snow shovel

'Any damn fool can be uncomfortable'

Commando School Instructor

Living out of doors in winter calls for a certain determination. It's always perfectly possible, but never exactly easy, and is therefore one more area which calls for plenty of technique. The aim is to be comfortable, for if you are comfortable you are safe, and since comfort means different things to different people, this aim can be set at a personal level. If you are comfortable you are probably doing the right thing.

The first point worth making is that in most countries there is no real need to camp out in winter unless you want to. Almost every hill or mountain area in the world possesses a hut or refuge system ideal for winter touring and used for just that purpose by winter *aficionados* who enjoy winter travel even more with a snug base available at the end of each day.

Huts

The Mountain Bothies Association, the Club Alpin Français (CAF), the Adirondack Mountain Club in New England, the Youth Hostels Association, the Touring Club de France, the Austrian Alpine Club, and the Den Norske Turistforening (DNT) are just a few of the many outdoor organisations throughout the world which maintain huts in mountain areas. The DNT is perhaps the most refined of these and their huts set a standard which all others might aspire to equal and can serve as our example. The DNT run three types of hut; there are staffed lodges, rather like small hotels, which are open for overnight stops and serve meals; self-service chalets stocked with bedding and provisions, which are regularly replenished; and finally unstaffed huts, fully equipped with all but food.

Some of these huts are open to the public at large; some, in theory anyway, are reserved for members. In practice no one is turned away, especially in winter, and most of the organisations have reciprocal arrangements with outdoor organisations in other countries, so that membership of one such organisation at home affiliates the member to similar organisations abroad.

In the UK, good organisations to join with international connections are the YHA, Trevelyn House, St Albans, Herts., and the UK section of the Austrian Alpine Club, Longcroft House, Fretherne Road, Welwyn Garden City, Herts. The British Mountaineering Club is in the course of issuing a 'mountain passport', which will enable members to share hut facilities with the CAF and other climbing organisations throughout the world. Apart from access to information, which is always useful, membership entitles the member to lower hut fees and grants permission to reserve a place in advance, which is again especially useful in winter when huts may be crowded or closed. A list of outdoor organisations is included in the Appendices.

Quite apart from these organisations, most hill areas contain small hotels which are open all the year round, where the proprietors become especially friendly in winter, when the summer crowds have gone. They can provide the perfect base for day walking or ski-touring forays into the surrounding countryside.

There is, in short, usually no need to camp out unless you want to, and certainly on the initial winter trips, the use of such facilities can be recommended.

Starting out

Winter has its own challenges, but it would be a retrograde step for any experienced three-season walker or camper to retreat to his own back garden and learn all the ropes from the very beginning. On the other hand, piling in all the gear and heading out into the deep winter wild is equally inadvisable. Ideally, the winter novice should make his or her first few trips with a more experienced group of friends. One trip isn't enough. Go several times so that winter problems can occur, and be coped with, when the others' knowledge and experience is available.

Failing that, a number of day trips, extending to overnight and

weekend trips, is advisable before setting off for a full one- to
two-week winter trip.

The winter day

The winter day is short. Summer campers are used to waking at
dawn, say around 0530 hours, and enjoying evenings which last
until 2100 hours. In winter it is rarely light enough to move before
0730 hours, and it is essential to be settled in for the night by one
hour before dark, say by 1500 hours in the depth of winter. This, if
you are on the move by 0800 hours, means a travelling day of some
7 hours, less stops, and a night of about 14 hours (1700 to 0700
hours). These timings are clearly flexible, but over the last two
winters I have noticed that in spite of all declared intentions we
were rarely on the move before 0900 hours and we were in our
sleeping bags by 1700 hours and stayed there, apart from short trips
outside, until someone lit the stove for the morning brew at about
0700 hours.

These timings impose their own restraints. You need to be
companionable and have a routine within the group. You must
accept the inevitable curtailment of distance. It is perfectly possible
to cover 48 km. (30 miles) a day on cross-country skis provided you
are fit and lightly equipped, with an equally fit companion, and
heading for a lodge or hostel where the evening preparation consists
of removing the skis and heading for the bar. In a group with loaded
rucksacks, and needing to find a pitch and settle in for the night
before dark, 24 km. (15 miles) is a more sensible distance. I set 24
km. (15 miles) a day as my winter maximum on skis and cut it down
according to the weather and the terrain.

In walking, while it again depends on ground cover and terrain,
about half the summer distance for similar terrain should be about
right. Your own experience and fitness will eventually enable you to
judge just how far you can go, and the wise traveller errs on the side
of caution, and pitches early.

Refuge in the Vercors, French Alps

A pitch here will be warmer than the valley floor.

Don't pitch next to a stream, it might rise.

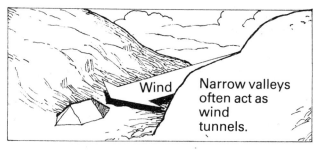

Wind

Narrow valleys often act as wind tunnels.

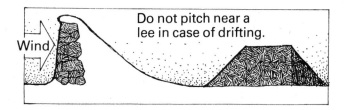

Wind

Do not pitch near a lee in case of drifting.

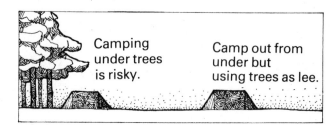

Camping under trees is risky.

Camp out from under but using trees as lee.

Selecting a pitch

In winter the traveller should always be looking for good pitches. Those you find too early in the day on the way out may come in handy on the way back, or useful in case you have to retreat, and are worth noting on the map. It is also a maxim that you will find the perfect pitch about a hundred metres *past* the point at which you finally stopped, and one of the winter traveller's favourite diversions towards the end of the day is the argument which develops as to the merits and demerits of every point you pass. Since the precious minutes of daylight are ticking away, this discussion cannot be too prolonged. If you find a mutually acceptable pitch at 1500 hours, use it. Don't fritter away the daylight hoping to find an even better one later on.

The ideal pitch in any season will be on level ground, sheltered from the wind and with access to water, but in winter these basic requirements need some amplification. Cold air flows down a slope, so that half way up a hill will be warmer than on the valley floor. A lee shelter from the wind is fine in summer, but in winter, if you are too close to the windbreak, driving snow will settle and bury you in a drift, so move away from it. Water must be accessible without the need to venture out on to ice.

Narrow valleys can be wind-tunnels for cold air or paths for avalanches. Camping under trees can be risky as extreme cold or heavy snow can break off branches or, more likely, dump lumps of snow on your tent or stove. The ideal pitch rarely exists, so look for a large enough level spot, out of the direct force of the wind, not in a hollow and not under trees, and without any obvious dangers from falling stones or avalanches.

Settling in

One of the secrets of winter warmth is activity. An active body is a warm body, and if you can be warm when you get into your sleeping bag, you will tend to stay warm. Do not idle about at the campsite and chill down. The best way to avoid this happening is to have a routine, which you adopt, individually and as a group, as soon as you stop, with the object of having the pitch prepared, the tent erected, and a meal on, in the shortest possible time. Everyone should have an allotted task and get on with it, without any need for bone-chilling chatter around the dumped packs.

Preparing the pitch
If the snow cover is light and shallow, it is as well to remove it, and pitch the tent directly on the bare ground. Light snow can be scraped away with a shovel, boots or skis. If the snow cover is deeper, the first task is to pack it down firmly, stamping down the surface first with the skis, then treading it even firmer with the boots. Snow trodden in this way will melt and then freeze into a firm platform. Any bumps or lumps will be permanent and hard to lie on, so flatten them with the shovel before you pitch the tent, taking care to prepare an even surface.

If you have bivvy bags or space blankets they can now be spread out on the surface in the area *under* the groundsheet. In this way they serve various useful purposes. Firstly, this is useful insulation. Secondly, heat from the occupied tent will soften the ground and make for mud. Mud on the groundsheet gets on to the tent. Thirdly, when you get up in the morning and the groundsheet cools it may freeze and stick to the ground. Pulling it free will sooner or later destroy the proofing. It is essential to reduce the amount of wet or snow tracked into the tent, so use your bivvy bag or space blanket to provide a 'doormat' in the porch, outside the main tent, where you can remove boots or dust off snow.

Erecting the tent
Careful pitching is essential in winter. Pitch the tent either sideways to the wind or angled into it. There is dispute between outdoor people on this point, some maintaining that tents should be pitched with the back to the wind, or even facing into it; in part it depends on the tent design. I feel that a billowing tent is not very restful to sleep in and since both exits on a ridge tent are needed the back is equally exposed. Clearly, it depends on the design of the tent, but for the ridge tent or tunnel tent sideways pitching seems to offer the best advantage.

Some tents can be pitched fly first, and if your tent has this feature, pitch the fly and get it down tight, using the extra guy loops to peg it closely to the ground. Pay particular attention to the fit of the inner, re-pitching it several times if necessary, until it is firmly in place and *the inner walls do not touch the fly at any point*. Time spent getting this right will pay dividends later on in minimising condensation.

Pegs and poles

Pegs and poles both present problems in winter. Firstly, metal poles and pegs get very cold, and in sub-zero temperatures should only be handled wearing gloves. Some campers tape the centre sections of poles with masking tape to cut down the chill factor. If the tent has a snow valance this can be weighted with snow or rocks.

Poles placed directly on snow will, unless the snow is very shallow or very hard, start to sink as soon as the guys are tightened, so wise campers carry a pair of flat metal discs which are tucked under the poles for extra support. Winter campers need a variety of pegs; straight steel pegs for hard ground or ice, serrated pegs for the wet, good long wooden pegs for soft snow. In really soft snow it may be necessary to dig down to the earth below to plant the peg, and use ice axes or ski poles as main guys. Pegs can be frozen-in by spilling water on them and by stamping the snow firm all around them.

Deadmen

A 'deadman' is a flat metal plate which is buried in the snow to act as a belay point, but winter campers can use normal pegs, buried sideways and frozen-in, or small logs and branches, or even a stuff-sack packed full of snow; all are useful 'deadmen'. One or two can serve on main guys. In this case bring the guy-rope knot to the surface so that the guy can be retrieved in the morning without the need to excavate the 'deadmen', which may, like frozen tent pegs, need to be extracted with an ice axe.

Moving in

While all this is going on, the party members must keep busy, fetching water, digging a lee wall, putting on a brew, anything rather than just waiting about getting cold. Once the site is prepared and the tent is up, the campers can move in. Clear the snow away from

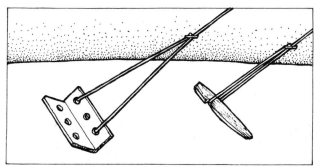

Various types of deadman

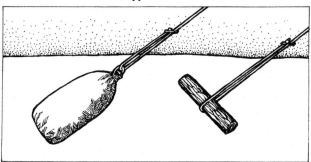

inside the porches, and either shovel it into a draught-wall or pile it around the valances. Aim for a tidy pitch. Mats should be deployed, sleeping bags laid out to 'loft' and sacks unpacked.

The rule is to complete all necessary outdoor preparations before moving into the tent. Brush as much snow as possible from the clothes and boots with a switch cut from a bush or with a small broom. Keep as much snow as possible out of the tent. Finally, fill and light cooking stoves outside, well away from the tent. It is better to cook outside if at all possible, but cooking outside is rarely practical in winter, and it is usually necessary to cook inside the tent porch.

Cooking

In winter the camp cook faces three fresh problem areas:

1. Difficulties with lighting stoves.
2. Water supplies.
3. Need for adequate calorie intake.

The experienced winter traveller will not do much cooking during the day. Long stops chill you and the effort of preparing a hot meal at midday will undo any benefit you can derive from it. The main meals are taken at breakfast and in the evening, with the object of providing calories for energy during the day and warmth at night. On the other hand it is important to eat during the day and drink plenty of fluids.

Food and calories

In winter, for daily heat and energy, the traveller needs to take in about 5000 calories, and a good balance of protein, carbohydrates and fats. Protein, in particular, is essential and it is worth noting that those who live in very cold climates, like the Eskimo, are great meat-eaters and need lots of protein to stay warm.

In winter the body is working hard simply to keep warm and this, plus the energy consumed in walking or cross-country skiing, means that the body's energy bank must be constantly topped up throughout the day.

Apart from aiming at an overall intake of 5000-plus calories, the winter camper must get the elements right. Aim for around:

1. 45% protein.
2. 35% carbohydrates.
3. Only 20% fats.
4. Plus some 'roughage' and fruit.

Take in protein and fats at the start of the day for breakfast, to give your body a good energy base, eating eggs, muesli, cheese, milk, to provide them. During the day take in some carbohydrate by eating sweets, sugar, glucose, cake, chocolate, to give a quick boost before you start to flag. Eat regularly and drink often, but try and avoid very cold water which draws heat from the stomach, and coffee, which is a diuretic and will just make you thirsty.

There is no need to get too concerned about this, although drawing up a good, well balanced meal programme is an enjoyable pre-trip task. Just take plenty of food, eat regularly and drink a lot.

Breakfast should be a filling meal of oatmeal porridge, muesli, even a stew or soup if you can face it. Frying food is not a good idea in winter. Cleaning a pan of frozen fat is a difficult task, although you can use crusty snow to remove most of it. Whatever you eat, eat plenty, and be sure to fill your water bottle. If you have a vacuum flask fill it with tea or hot soup for a trail lunch.

During the day, eat and drink often. Chocolate, glucose sweets, fudge and Kendal Mint Cake are all good for quick energy boosts, but above all drink plenty. Travelling in cold dry air, you are dehydrating fast.

Dehydrated foods
The evening meal needs to be a big one, with lots of soup and stew, some sort of pudding, and lots of tea. Long evenings are the times that tempt the traveller to pass the time drinking tea, but too much of this inevitably leads to the need for chilly night-time excursions, so try not to drink too much once you are inside for the night. Eating warm food is a real pleasure in winter and the introduction of good high-calorie freeze-dried foods from such companies as Mountain House, Raven and Springlow is an added boon. All these need is the addition of hot water, and they may be eaten from the packet. One-pot meals are clearly useful, particularly if all you must do to reconstitute the food is to add hot water. In practice reconstituting AFD (Accelerated Freeze-Dried) food can take a fair while. Some winter travellers tip the AFD food into a vacuum flask, top it up with hot water at lunch-time and have a hot, well reconstituted stew ready by the time they stop. Check this idea out carefully for there are two snags. Firstly, the expanding food may be too big for the flask and spill out, or secondly, the reconstituted food may be hard to extract through the narrow neck of the flask.

AFD food can become very unpalatable after a few days, and

fresh food or a few tins obtained along the way or even carried, in spite of their weight, can be a nice change.

The rule is to keep it simple. Stick to one-pot meals, lots of trail snacks, and plenty of fluids.

Stoves
Some outdoor books, especially American ones, make a great play about lighting open fires for warmth and cooking. This practice is increasingly deplored because of the environmental damage. It is also not very effective, since making a fire in the snow is hard work and makes for slow cooking. Use a petrol or paraffin stove, and stick to one-pot meals.

Winter tips for stoves are as follows:

1. Fill and light the stove outside, well away from the tent.
2. If the stove lacks a windshield, make one, or shield the flame with your pack or tools.
3. Place the stove firmly on an insulating surface like a piece of karrimat or your shovel, not on the bare snow.
4. All cook-pots should have lids. Use spare heat, in upturned lids for example, to warm water or melt snow.
5. If the stove is still burning, boil some water or melt some snow.

Finally, be wary of the effect of stove fumes and lack of oxygen in enclosed tents and snow-holes. This can lead to asphyxiation, so open up your tent when the stove is on. Using leaded fuels, such as 2-star petrol, is also unwise on a long-term basis. Use unleaded petrol (white gas), cook outside the tent or in the porch, and beware of condensation from steam and heated air.

Water
The importance of drinking plenty of water in winter can hardly be overemphasised. You will, in any event, get very thirsty, but finding water in winter is not always easy. Standpipes get turned off, streams are under the snow or frozen over. Melting snow is a tedious process as even a full pot of snow leaves a very shallow puddle when melted, and this takes a lot of precious fuel. If you

must melt snow, start with a small amount and add more as it melts. This process will be much quicker if you start with a little water in the bottom of the pot. Better still, melt ice, smashing it up small with the ice axe or crampons before putting it in the pot.

My routine is to start the day by drinking as much as I can of slightly warm water. I then top up my water bottle and place it inside my pack, at the back, where my body heat can reach it, enclosing the bottle in a cut-off sock. In sub-zero weather, put the bottle upside down, so that ice forms in the bottom rather than at the neck, and lightly grease the screw-top with petroleum jelly. A frozen top is frustrating and hard to open.

Take every possible chance to drink, but remember that icy water straight from a stream will chill the stomach. It is better to drink tepid water from the bottle and then top it up. Winter walkers and skiers will soon notice that they pass very little water which will give some idea of how much fluid is lost to the body by perspiration and evaporation. A daily salt tablet is recommended to replace body salts lost in this way.

Utensils
Cold metal can stick to the skin in sub-zero temperatures, so use plastic for mugs and plates, or tape any metal parts you are liable to grab absent-mindedly. Be especially careful, when filling your stove, not to spill petrol on your skin. The extra heat loss caused when the chilled fuel evaporates can cause frostnip or even frostbite if the temperature is really low. I always use a funnel and hold that by the pot-grab to keep my hands well clear.

Cleaning
Bacteria do not thrive in the cold but it pays to clean the pots and plates with frozen snow after use and wipe them dry. Rubbish, such as wrappers, can be kept in plastic bags until you find a proper waste-disposal point. Do not bury your rubbish in the snow. It will simply be preserved until spring, and litter in the wilderness can take years to disappear. According to an outdoor magazine survey of litter:

1. Aluminium tags and cans last 80 years.
2. Plastic film lasts 20 years.
3. Wool socks last 1-5 years.
4. Orange peel lasts up to 5 months.
5. Plastic-coated containers last 5 years.

The lesson is plain. If you pack it in, pack it out, in winter as in summer.

Nightime
After pitching the tent and cooking a meal, the time has come to settle down for the night. A good night's sleep is essential but remember that during the night the wind can get up and the weather can change. It pays, therefore, to be well organised before you settle down to sleep.

Check around outside to see that all pegs and guys are holding. If double guying has not been done and it looks necessary, do it now. Clear away any snow from the fly, and repack any spare items back in the rucksack. The sack can usually be left in the porch, but certain items should be kept inside the tent, if they are to stay unfrozen throughout the night. Boots will freeze, so I put mine inside a stuff-sack, wrapped in my over-trousers, and use it as a pillow.

Water bottles, in their socks, go between the sleeping bags. The torch goes inside my sleeping bag where I can find it, and the batteries will stay warm. Finally, I put my camp boots, spare sweater, hat and cagoule at my side, ready to put on for nocturnal excursions. For one reason or another I always have to get up in the night. If it is snowing it will be necessary to go out during the night to remove the snow from the tent, so a watch system may be needed. Ice coating the tent, or shutting all the vents, can lead to anoxia, so check your ventilation and have the snow shovel to hand.

Dry clothing
Eventually, your clothing is going to get wet. It depends on the temperature, the degree and types of precipitation, and your skill with shell clothing and zips, but sooner or later increasing dampness will cause a problem and somehow or other you must get your

clothes dry.

Some people believe you should sleep in wet or at least damp clothes and so dry them for use in the day. Current opinion, and mine, favours putting on dry clothes at night, saving them for sleeping and for use in emergencies. Putting on damp clothes in the morning is disagreeable, but they soon warm up under a cagoule and windproof trousers. While you are 'wet-warm' you are in no danger, but if you become 'wet-cold', and the weather turns nasty, then hypothermia is a definite possibility and dry clothing a useful weapon against it. It must be said again that dampness in winter is the real enemy, so try and dry any damp clothing during the day on the outside of the rucksack, or inside the tent at night.

Heaters

There are small heaters suitable for backpacking such as the ALP gas lantern, which is light (350 gm.) (12 oz.) and pumps out a great deal of heat. It also produces a great deal of condensation and, by and large, heaters are not all that useful in a small winter tent.

Before all the clothing and sleeping gear gets damp and unusable you will have to stop and have a drying session. Put this off for as long as possible by good technique, but face the fact that dry clothing is important.

Evening tasks

There are those who rest up for a few hours and travel on after moonrise, but this is hardly an everyday event, although it is very enjoyable, and can be one way of clawing back distance on firm night-time snow if the day has proved a slow one.

On a normal night the group can expect to spend 14 hours or so in the tent and, except for emergencies, may not need to emerge.

This is the time for a little reading, for re-checking the timings, and preparing and checking route cards for the morrow. Carry out any small repairs, and doctor any blisters. It may be possible to rearrange loads, and as a general rule use the night not just to rest, but to get the group ready for another day tomorrow.

Tent maintenance

Apart from chatting, reading, working out the next day's route on
the map and drinking tea, with or without a nip of the hard stuff,
winter campers will need to spend a great deal of time keeping the
tent tidy and in good order. Try as you will, snow and spindrift will
infiltrate, and condensation forms on the walls, so that fairly
constant mopping up with a cloth is necessary. Good ventilation will
help to reduce this, especially when using a stove or candle, but
some condensation is inevitable.

   If it starts or continues to snow, it may be necessary to turn out
from time to time to scrape heavy snow off the roof or from the
entrances.

Sleeping

If you get into the bag warm and eat a good meal, you should stay
warm. If you feel cold put on your hat or turn up your hood. If you
still feel cold do a few isometric exercises, clenching and relaxing
the muscles, and put on any spare clothing you have or can borrow.
Spare clothing is to be used when necessary, not just carried about.
If you still can't get warm eat something, prepare a drink, put on
still more clothing and wonder if you might have a touch of
hypothermia. Some people, like myself, sleep warm, and pump out
lots of heat, while others have difficulty resisting the cold. It
depends on the individual metabolism, but good technique will
enable any sensibly equipped camper to enjoy a good night's sleep.

Striking camp

In the morning try to be awake and, if possible, fed just before
daylight. Have a good breakfast, and as soon as there is enough light
to see what you are doing, get up, dress and start packing. Frost will
have frozen on the fly, if not on the inner, and it must be shaken off.
Put the tent and the fly into separate bags, and try to keep at least
the inner dry. This is easier if the inner can be struck in the shelter
of the fly and you have placed a space blanket down for ground
cover. Remove and count all the pegs, and check the site area
carefully for missing objects. If it is snowing it is very easy to lose
small items. I find it best to leave the bivvy bag or space blanket on

the ground and place everything on it, for a final check. I then give the things a quick wipe over with a cloth before opening the rucksack and storing them away. Try to avoid constantly opening the rucksack as this lets in damp.

The important point in the morning is to do everything you can do from the warmth of the bag, and once you are up move fast. The object is the same as for pitching, to keep warm by keeping active. With good management the group can be packed up and on the move within one hour of waking. Take your rubbish with you and leave nothing behind.

Keeping clean

No doubt there are hardy souls who start the winter's day with a stiff shave and a roll in the snow, but I have never met one. Huts usually have adequate washing facilities, but tent life tends to be more uncivilised.

I settle for cleaning the teeth and, later on, when I feel more alive, a quick hands-and-face wash with a warm wet flannel. Shaving is easier now that I carry a battery-powered razor, and after each wash I anoint my face and lips with barrier cream. With luck, and weather permitting, it is possible to manage some kind of body wash over a few days, often a bit at a time. You can get fairly 'doggy' in the winter, but since it's cold and everyone else is in the same state, no one seems to care. That long, hot shower at the end of the trip is bliss, though.

Latrines

The winter traveller passes very little water, and this, therefore, presents no problem. More complicated matters call for courage, and most winter travellers accept constipation as a fact of life. When all else fails get out of the wind, hack out a hold in the ground with the ice axe, and act fast. Never foul the campsite or anywhere even close to running water and, if possible, burn the paper before covering the hole. Paper tissues are better than toilet paper, and since noses tend to run in cold weather are usually readily to hand.

Repairs and maintenance
We have touched on this before, but gear failure can be disastrous. Winter weather is not especially hard on good gear, but faults in equipment cannot usually be left until you return to base. A jammed door zip may make your tent uninhabitable if it is snowing, so a repair kit should be carried on a group basis. It should contain as a minimum:

1. Six large safety pins.
2. A roll of rip-stop nylon tape.
3. Needle and thread.
4. Thin nylon line.

Once you return to base, or if you stop for the day in a warm shelter, have a complete sort-out of gear and a general clean-up as soon as possible, and certainly before the next day. Gear, especially nylon tents, takes some time to dry out, and once metal items start to rust they will continue to do so. We once stopped at a monastery in Spain after two wet, cold days on the hill. We were soaked to the skin and all our gear was muddy, but after a night draped over every radiator in the place, all our clothing and equipment was dry and usable again and we could press on, as good as new. I recommend that winter travellers miss no opportunity to keep their equipment in good order and dry it out.

Winter living is and must be SIMPLE. Life is reduced to the essentials, but these essentials *are* essential:

1. Learn how to use your clothing and equipment properly.
2. Avoid dampness from perspiration and precipitation.
3. Eat a lot and eat often.
4. Drink a lot of water.
5. Don't attempt too much.
6. Watch the weather.

These are the essentials. All the rest are means to achieving them, and the end result is to make winter living safe, comfortable and fun.

'Simplification of means, and elevation of ends is the goal'

Thoreau

For much of the time, over most of the terrain, and anywhere off snow, the winter traveller can manage perfectly well in boots. In winter it is better to wear a heavier pair than one might choose for a similar trip in summer. You should give them a good waxing, especially in the welt and along the seams, and wear gaiters as well to help keep the wet out but, up to a point, boots will do.

The point is reached on snow, at about ankle depth. Walking on snow deeper than this, especially if the surface is breakable crust, is very tiring, very slow and, if the snow has drifted deeper along fences and in gullies, eventually impossible. At this point the traveller must take to skis or snow-shoes, and here winter travelling begins.

Skis or snow-shoes
The choice lies between the following three types:

1. Cross-country or Nordic skis.
2. Ski-mountaineering or Alpine skis.
3. Snow-shoes.

The choice is decided by the terrain, by the skier's experience and ability with the equipment and, to a certain extent, by fashion and availability.

Terrain
In simple terms, cross-country Nordic skis with toe bindings are chiefly used on rolling, hilly, rather than mountainous, terrain and

Ski tourers near Voss, Norway

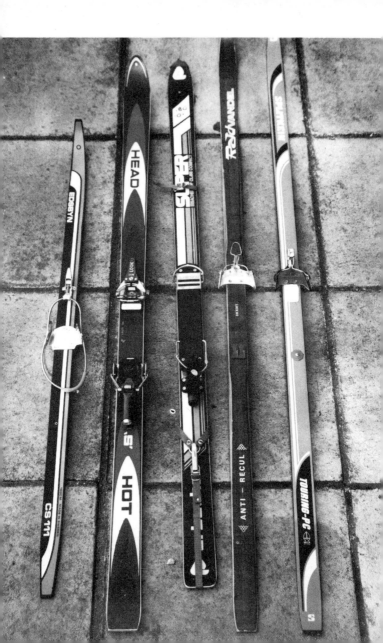

at moderate heights.

Ski-mountaineering skis, which are Alpine skis with special bindings, are for high mountain work on off-piste, deep snow.

Snow-shoes are a North American creation and were originally used by the American Indians for winter hunting. They are slowly coming into use in Europe and are fairly popular in Scandinavia. Their chief advantage is that the technique of snow-shoeing is easy to learn, and for close bush country, or even for moving about a snowy campsite, they can be very useful. A small round pair of the type the French call 'raquettes' would be useful equipment for any snow camper.

For covering any real distance, though, the traveller must use skis. Both types of skis present problems, because to use them properly and enjoyably does demand skill and technique. Cross-country or Nordic skiing is fairly easy to learn and may be developed to a touring level in about a week, but anyone going ski-mountaineering must first have a good grasp of downhill skiing on prepared pistes, up to Intermediate standard, with some experience of deep snow skiing, and be able to do reliable parallel turns. Without such experience and techniques, ski-mountaineering is not an option open to the winter traveller.

Nomenclature

One of the problems encountered in writing about ski-touring, which is the general term for any off-piste or off-loipe work (loipe is a prepared cross-country track), is the multiplicity of terms. Not only do different countries use different terms, they use the same terms but mean different things. This can cause considerable confusion.

Cross-country skiing, for example, is referred to as Nordic, Langlauf, XC, Ski de fond, Sci-da-fondo, ski-rambling, ski-wandering and ski-touring. Ski-mountaineering is *also* called ski-touring, and there are those who go ski-touring but in Alpine

Skis: (left to right) Ski with cable binding, Alpine ski, Ski mountaineering-ski, General touring ski, Loipe ski country, and wearing cross-country skis! It makes for confusion, so for the purpose of this book let me define my terms as follows:

1. Cross-country skiing will be referred to as Nordic skiing. This means skiing on Nordic skis with toe-bindings, over moderate rolling, hilly terrain.
2. Ski-mountaineering is skiing in mountain country, off-piste on Alpine skis with ski-mountaineering bindings.
3. Ski-touring will specifically refer to off-loipe skiing on Nordic skis. If I use the term for high mountain skiing as in (2) above, I will say so.

Whole books have been written on both types of skiing and ski-touring, several by me. In this chapter I propose to give an outline of each method, describing the equipment, the techniques and the advantages they offer to the winter traveller in the hills, and off prepared tracks. It is my firm conviction that no winter traveller has mastered the winter environment, or, more important, can enjoy it to the full, without using snow-shoes and at least one sort of skis. They increase the traveller's mobility and range considerably, and much of the winter countryside can only be entered using skis or snow-shoes.

Nordic skiing
Nordic skis have been around for several thousand years. They were and still are used by the Scandinavian people simply to get about in a land that has snow cover for eight months of the year, and most Scandinavian children can ski as soon as they can walk.

Nordic skiing is an ideal sport for the summer walker and backpacker, as the natural extension of his or her summer activities. Moreover, Nordic equipment is light and reasonably cheap to buy, while the techniques are simple and easy to learn.

Equipment
Nordic skiing has been booming for several years now, and the range of skis, boots and ancillary equipment is expanding and changing constantly.

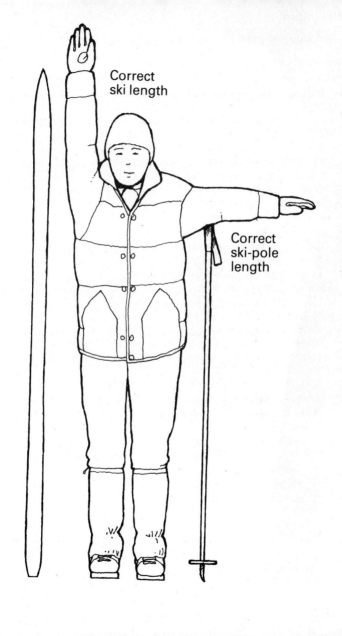

Correct
ski length

Correct
ski-pole
length

Nordic skis

The Nordic ski today is usually made of hickory, fibreglass, or various plastics such as polyethylene. Except for cosmetic purposes on the upper surfaces, wood is dying out. Nordic skies are long, light and narrow and have a high arch or camber. To judge the correct length for you, hold the hand above the head and choose the ski that is wrist high.

Nordic skis come in four broad types; Racing, Light Touring, General Touring and Mountain. The first two are used for competitive work, or day touring on prepared loipe, but the winter traveller is mainly interested in the last two types.

General Touring skis are wider than the Light Touring type and are fairly flexible at the tips for deep snow work. They may have full or half-length steel edges but more often have edges in plastic or lignostone, a material made from compressed beech. General Touring skis will turn better if they are slightly 'waisted' or, in skiing parlance, have 'side cut'.

The weight per pair will be between 2 and 2.5 kilos (4 and 5 lb.). Suitable touring skis will be 52–60 mm. wide at the waist and stiffly cambered. Extra camber is necessary on General Touring skis, for the skier's weight is increased by a pack. If the ski is too soft, the waist will be depressed and the tip and tail of the ski can lift off the snow.

Mountain skis will always have steel edges for cutting into steeper icy slopes, and are often slightly shorter than the General Touring variety by, say, 5–10 cm. Good skiers can use Nordic skis in terrain that verges on ski-mountaineering country, but it calls for good technique. The winter traveller, then, will choose General Touring or Mountain skis. There are plenty of good makes, Trak, Bonna, Splitkein, Skilom, to name but a few. The big decision, apart from type, is to wax or not to wax.

Waxes

Whole books have been written on the subject of Nordic ski waxes. Traditionally, ski waxes were used on the base of Nordic skis to provide 'grip' for climbing and 'glide' for downhill and on the flat. Since these aims are contradictory, choosing the right wax for any

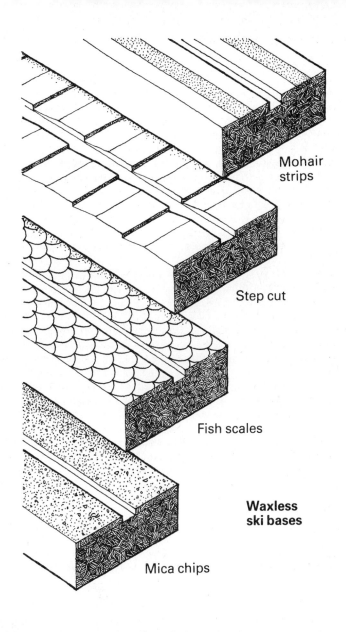

Mohair strips

Step cut

Fish scales

Waxless ski bases

Mica chips

given snow condition is crucial and calls for a certain amount of judgement. During the day, snow conditions change, particularly for the ski-tourer, who is travelling across country and will inevitably encounter different types of snow. It is therefore necessary to renew or change the wax.

Many people enjoy waxing but the introduction of the non-wax ski certainly gave Nordic skiing, and particularly the touring side, a great boost in popularity as it removed one major source of hassle, for many people found waxing and re-waxing a terrible chore.

People are perverse, though, and as more and more people take up Nordic skiing and become more experienced, so waxing regains popularity.

Non-wax skis provide 'grip' in various ways: with mohair strips set in the base; by serrating the centre section of the base into 'step-cut' or 'fish-scale' patterns; or by coating the base with mica flakes. All work adequately well for touring, but inevitably with some loss of performance when compared with the waxed models, a loss which many tourers accept as an exchange for freedom from waxing problems.

A fairly recent innovation is the introduction of the 'wide-range wax', which requires the skier to decide only if the snow is wet (above freezing) or dry (below freezing) before applying the appropriate wax and getting adequate 'grip' and help with the 'glide'. As a convinced non-wax ski-tourer for years, I have now used 'wide-range' waxes for the last two winters and found them a most useful and effective compromise between relying on non-wax bases and going in for the full waxing routine.

To sum up, my advice is that the winter camper, walker or backpacker, taking to Nordic skis, should buy or (initially) hire waxless General Touring or Mountain skis, with three-pin Nordic Norm bindings, and use wide-range waxes on tip and tail, especially for extra glide. A spare ski-tip can be carried for use in the event of a ski breaking on the trail.

Bindings
Nordic skis are fitted with toe-bindings, which are matched to the boot in standard fitting sizes, or 'Norms'. The winter traveller is

interested in either the 50-mm. Touring Norm or the 75-mm. Nordic Norm, although this last one is also available in 71-mm. and 79-mm. widths. Provided the 'Norm' is the same any boot will fit any binding, regardless of the foot size of the wearer. These toe-bindings enable the skier to move on the flat and climb hills. The heel is free and grips the ski only by friction on a small stud or 'popper' which is fixed to the ski at a point measured to meet the boot-heel.

Cable bindings, which can clamp the heel down for the descent, are still sometimes recommended for ski-touring, but I have not seen any in use for several years now. Cable bindings will not release in a fall, and I believe they are both unnecessary and dangerous, for even a minor injury could have far-reaching consequences when touring in the back country. Heel-locators, which are devices to hold the heel on the ski and prevent it side-slipping off in a turn, may have some use in deep snow, and can be recommended for touring. Cross country bindings get tough treatment, and it is advisable to carry some spares, a few screws and some epoxy glue, in case a binding breaks.

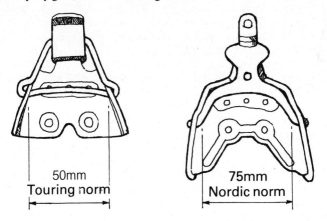

Trak 50 norm sole and binding (overleaf left)
Cross-country boot with heel clamps (overleaf right)

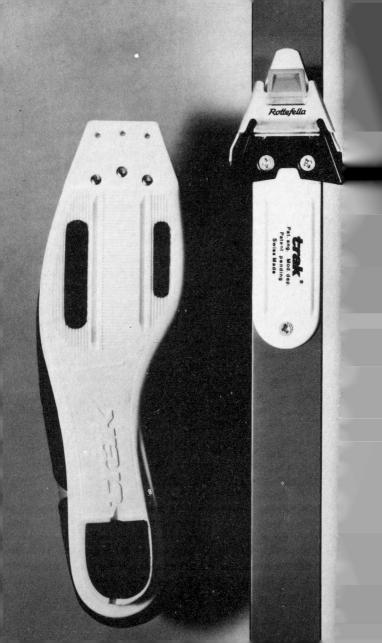

The choice between Touring and Nordic Norms is up to the skier. The Touring Norm is said to be marginally faster, but the Nordic Norm is more widely available and would be my personal choice at present.

Poles

Nordic poles are long and should reach up into the armpit, like a crutch. They are made from bamboo or aluminium, and need good leather grips. The snap-on baskets need either large snow-shedding holes in the rim or, even better, one of the newly developed cone or butterfly shapes, which shed the snow and do not drag on the snow surface during the forward swing.

Boots

Unlike the stiff, heavy Alpine skiing or ski-mountaineering boots, Nordic boots are light, flexible and usually lined. They admit the wet so they should be worn with gaiters or in deep winter with synthetic lined 'boot-gloves', or overshoes, which fit over the boot and have holes on the soles to take the pin-binding. Touring boots are cut *above* the ankle and have a sewn-in tongue.

Clothing

The clothing as described in Chapter 2 is perfectly adequate for off-loipe ski-touring. There are fashionable, well cut Nordic ski suits available, which are comfortable to wear, and indeed I use one for loipe work and day touring. On longer tours I have normal winter walking clothing, which is more versatile. A Rohan Helenca salopette or breeches and a fibre-pile jacket is ideal, backed up when I stop with a down vest and shell clothing. Nordic skiing is hot work, and to reduce perspiration and the dreaded damp the skier must wear as little as possible when skiing, while protecting the feet, ears and hands, and putting on warm clothing as soon as he or she stops. Strip off as much clothing as possible, though, before you start again.

Berghaus 55 litre ski-mountaineering sack

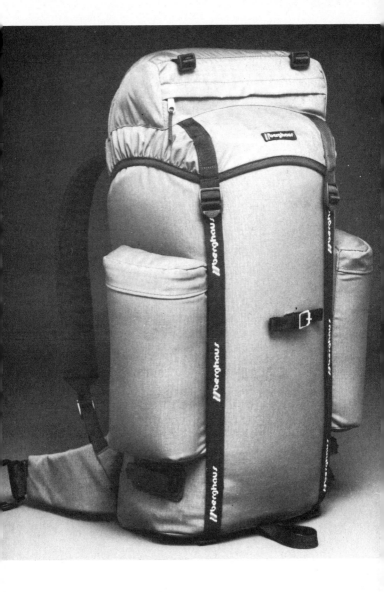

Ancillary equipment

Here again, but with some minor adjustments, the equipment outlined in Chapter 3 will do very well, as it was recommended with this sort of activity in mind. Weight and balance are clearly important, and wide side-pocketed rucksacks, in particular, are not suitable for extended tours as they impede the to-and-fro arm action of the skier. Use a long narrow sack with hip harness and a 'sternum' or chest strap. Straps, or pockets, for carrying the skis and poles are also useful. Rucksacks should be packed with the heavy items low at the bottom of the sack to improve balance, not high up in normal backpacking style. The total weight must be reduced by sharing out the loads as much as possible among the group as well as cutting equipment to the minimum. The Nordic skier will also need one or two extra items like a ski repair kit and some waxes, but these too can be carried on a 'group' basis.

Nordic techniques

Nordic technique is very basic, and comparatively easy to learn. Out with a group of absolute beginners in the Austrian Tyrol recently, we were going on 24-km. (15-mile) tours over moderate terrain after three days' instruction. Clearly, though, it depends on the terrain, and the novice skier would be well advised to stay away from steep, icy, narrow trails down through trees until he or she can control the speed and is able to turn and stop in any circumstances.

Diagonal stride

The basic technique in Nordic skiing is the diagonal stride, a simple extension of the normal walking movement. This is best learned on a practice loipe over flat terrain. Start with a normal walk, swinging the arms well forward and towards the rear, then gradually put more weight *over* the bent leading knee and start to glide. The poles are used more for balance than effort, and the basic diagonal stride action is a skating motion, pushing off the rear foot and gliding along in a series of rhythmic strides. Downhill running can be aided by pushing with both poles, while stopping relies almost entirely on the 'snow-plough' turn. For this, push out the backs of the skis, keep the tips together and go 'knock-kneed' to edge the skis.

The diagonal stride

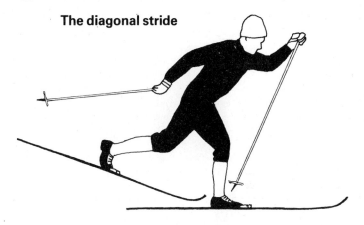

Turns

Putting weight on one or other of the skis will induce the 'snow-plough' position turn.

On open slopes the 'step' or 'skate' turn is employed. This consists of putting all the weight on one ski, lifting the other out at about 30° from the vertical fall line, transferring the weight to it, then bringing the skis together, repeating this action until you are parallel to the direct fall line and able to stop. The 'Telemark' turn is difficult with a full pack, and consists of pushing one ski well forward until the skier is virtually kneeling, while the other ski trails behind. The tip of the front ski is then angled in the required direction, left ski out for a turn to the right and vice-versa, and round you go.

Climbing

Climbing up is relatively easy on Nordic skis, for the bases, whatever the surface, will give sufficient grip for a direct climb to most slopes. If the slope is very steep or icy, it may be necessary to climb it in a series of diagonals, and use 'kick-turns' to change direction. The ability to handle side-stepping and herringbone ascents is also needed.

The snowplough position

Nordic skiing is growing in popularity with outdoor people for all these reasons: low price of equipment; simple techniques; and ease of learning. It is, however, a skilled sport, and requires a certain application. It has been called 'walking on skis', but experienced Nordic skiers regard this as a considerable oversimplification.

The winter traveller taking up Nordic skiing should allow for a good five days to learn and practise the basics and get even walking-fit muscles used to the strains of the Nordic technique. Stick to short tours on fairly level terrain until you feel happy with the diagonal stride, the snow-plough turn and stop, the skate turn and various methods of climbing. Lose no opportunity to practise Nordic touring skills on various snow surfaces and over ever steeper slopes.

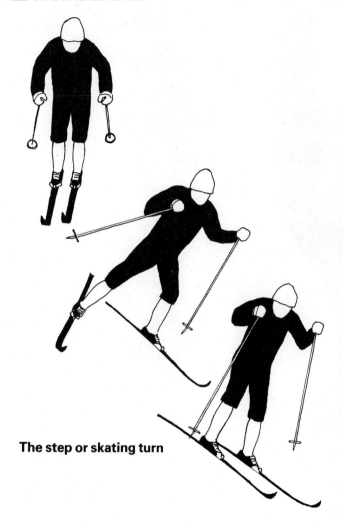

The step or skating turn

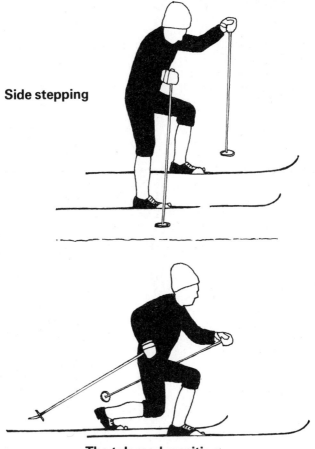

Side stepping

The telemark position

Ski-mountaineering
Ski-mountaineering pre-dates the introduction of Alpine lift systems and harks back to the days when skiers climbed for hours to

enjoy a heady few moments of descent on unpacked snow. Ski-mountaineers today tend to be either downhill skiers bored with the racetrack of the piste, or summer mountaineers extending their activities into winter, perhaps for the skiing, or perhaps as a means of getting up to the mountain to start a climb. It is fair to say again that the would-be ski-mountaineer must have good skiing abilities first, up to at least the Intermediate level, before attempting this challenging sport.

Skis

Most ski-mountaineers use normal downhill skis fitted with hinged ski-mountaineering bindings, but the ideal ski should be lighter, shorter and more 'soft' or flexible than that used for piste running. I use 185-mm. compacts on the piste, while for off-piste touring I use 175-mm. mid-length skis; these are much lighter and the flexible tips plane up the surface of the snow. Sharp steel edges are essential, for there is sure to be ice on the tops, and rounded edges will not give adequate grip on an icy traverse.

Bindings

Ski-mountaineering bindings have to do three things well. They must unlatch to allow the heel to rise for progress uphill and on the flat; they must clamp down securely for the descent; finally, they must have a reliable release mechanism in the event of a fall. Some ski-mountaineers still use Tempo or Silvretta cable bindings, but newer designs modelled on modern step-in or plate release bindings are available and must be recommended. Money spent on good bindings is never wasted. A friend of mine broke a wrist at St Moritz last year and the bill for setting it was over £300. Add on the cost which could occur to an injured ski-mountaineer far from the piste, the rescue, the transport (and the pain!) quite apart from the cost and difficulty of getting comprehensive insurance cover for ski-mountaineering and, from any standpoint, a good binding for ski-mountaineering is a good investment. Finding shops which stock good ski-mountaineering bindings is difficult, for this is still a minority sport. My advice is to buy and have them fitted in a mountain area, where a fair selection should be available and where

the ski-shop's mechanic knows his job. Marker, the Gertsch G700 and the Su-Matic are all good makes. Even if the skis have 'ski-stoppers', use an ankle strap. If you lose a ski in deep snow, it will plane along under the surface and you may never find it.

Boots

The ski-mountaineering boot today is a compromise between the stiff downhill boot, with 'flo-fit' lining and lots of clips, and the heavy stiff leather mountaineering boot. It should have a snow cuff, and a vibram sole for walking in the snow. The heel should be grooved or have a wide welt edge to hold the heel binding. Unlike the modern downhill boot, the ski-mountaineering boot should allow the skier to wear two pairs of socks, and should not be done up so tightly as to reduce circulation.

Poles

Normal Alpine poles will serve, but it is better if they have wider baskets which give better support in deep snow.

Skins

Where Nordic skiers use wax, mohair or step-cut configurations for grip, ski-mountaineers use skins. These were originally sealskin, as the name implies, but today are long, ski-wide strips of mohair which are strapped or glued (or both) to the base of the ski. These skins provide an amazing amount of grip for climbing even icy slopes, and are easily removed for the descent.

Harscheisen

Ski-crampons or Harscheisen are very like instep crampons. They fit under the boot and over the edge of the ski. They are used, like crampons, for getting over ice, usually in areas where there is a mixed surface of ice, snow crust and bare rock.

Clothing

The clothing outlined in Chapter 2 would be suitable, but the

Ski touring bindings. Rear: Toe binding. Foreground: Gertsch alpine binding ski-mountaineers might look with a more favourable eye on down, for at height the risk of rain lessens and, thanks to the lapse rate, it will certainly be colder.

Downhill ski suits are too hot for the climbing part of ski-mountaineering, so the skier should remember basic principles and opt for layered clothing. Removing as much as possible for the ascent and wrapping up well for the downhill sections is the best advice to follow.

Equipment

The ski-tourer, whether on Nordic or Alpine skis, and certainly in Europe, tends to use huts or mountain refuges. This means that the amount of kit can be sharply reduced, and the kit that remains can be shared out amongst the group. Windproofs, a sleeping bag, spare gloves and extra clothing and a pair of hut boots are the essentials. Food and other items depend on the aims of the trip and the facilities available en route.

Techniques

The would-be ski-mountaineer should be fit, and must be a competent downhill skier. Flogging up steep snow slopes carrying a pack, or traversing open ridges hour upon hour is hard work, and downhill running in unpacked snow is very different from running on prepared piste.

The skier should be up to SCGB Silver standard, and be able to ski in deep off-piste snow, using parallel turns. Most ski-mountaineering trips usually and wisely begin in a downhill resort, where the skier can spend a day or two running in unpacked snow on the edge of the piste, learning or revising the necessary touring techniques.

Off-piste skiing can be hard work, and depends very much on the snow state. If the snow is soft or powder the skis disappear, which is itself unnerving, and during turns the snow can exert pressure all over the ski, not just on the base and edges.

Learning deep-snow techniques really calls for a qualified instructor and a great deal of practice, but the basics are fairly straightforward, and can soon be grasped by a strong and competent skier.

Keep the weight evenly on both skis. The skier on a packed piste can turn by moving the weight sharply from one ski to the other. Try that in deep snow and the weighted ski just sinks. So how *do* you turn? It depends on the snow, but use a steep traverse, close to the fall line, weight evenly on the skis and a little back. It helps if the ski tips are in view, and keeping the weight back a little helps to keep the tips up.

> **To turn in deep snow, keep close to the fall line; lean back a little, keep the skis close together and use LOTS of flexing and extension when turning. DO NOT edge the ski or overweight one of them.**

Deep snow turns

Turning
Touring in deep snow calls for much more weighting and unweighting in the turns and for a very positive 'up and down' movement, and the skis should be banked to the snow in the turns, presenting the whole base rather than just the edge. One way to induce this banking is to raise the outer arm sharply, when unweighting. Deep snow skiing puts a real strain on the thigh muscles, and calls for exaggerated but accurate movement. The skis should be kept further apart than for piste running, and the weight

held to the rear so that when (not if) you run into heavier snow you are not thrown forward off balance, into a fall. If the snow is not too deep face the direction you are heading in on the traverse until just before you flex down for the turn, when you should swivel round to the fresh direction. This can be done by steering the skis uphill before the turn, but the effect is the same. This action puts, indeed requires, a twisting motion of the knees and ankles to turn the skis, but this is inevitable because you are skiing *through* snow rather than on it, and you must shift the snow away in order to turn. The closer the skier can keep to the fall line the better and easier the turns will be.

Stopping is also a problem in deep snow since the usual skidded stop turns will cause falls, if indeed they can be induced at all.

The answer is *anticipation* and uphill stem-swings, keeping the skis parallel, the weight a little back and then slowly swinging, pressing the ski tails out and down to turn uphill and stop.

Downhill skiers used to the groomed piste will find that the big problem is to move the skis at all. Downhill skiers use speed and 'edge' to turn. Ski-mountaineers must use legs and 'weight' to turn the whole ski. Resist the idea that the skis must be kept flat. Imagine that you are *waggling* them and use the pressure of snow building up against the bottom of the ski to take you round. It takes lots of practice, but it is a technique that any competent skier can acquire without undue difficulty.

Ski-touring
The following points hold good for Nordic skiing and ski-mountaineering. Ski-touring calls for a lot more than just a good grasp of Nordic or downhill skiing techniques. You should not go ski-touring on either sort of equipment until you are experienced at travelling in the winter hills, and ski-mountaineers, in particular, would be wise to follow known routes and take an experienced guide. It helps to be fit.

Ski-touring of either sort is hard work, and it is essential to use the clothing properly to reduce perspiration build-up. It is also essential that the group works as a group and stays together. If you are not going to stay together, why did you go together? Daily distance must allow for changeable weather and for a slow rate of progress. Speeding along leads to sweat and all the problems sweat inherits. It is essential to start slowly, conserve energy, replacing it with trail snacks, and hit a pace which:

1. Reduces perspiration.
2. Keeps the group together.
3. Achieves the objective.

Finally, a word about the snow. Snow will vary over height, distance, the course of the day, and according to the weather. The two nice sorts of snow for tourers are shallow or packed powder. The nasty sort of snow for touring is breakable crust, where the surface has thawed and frozen again, but is not up to supporting any weight, so that the skier is continually breaking through the crust into the soft heavy snow below, especially in the turns. Breakable crust is almost impossible to ski on. I recall having to abandon a beautiful downhill run and side-step because of the pain of smashing my shin-bones through the crust. If the snow is crusty start early in the day when it is freezing hard or ski in shadow out of the sun. Or give up.

Snow-shoes
In Canada and North America snow-shoes are very popular. In Europe they are much less common, though every winter sees them being used a little more, but for any mountain walk between November and April the walker will surely find places where snow-shoes would be useful. In Europe the most common type of snow-shoe is a simple aluminium circular hoop, not unlike the business end of a tennis racquet, with nylon webs and neoprene or canvas straps. This is a simplified form of the American Bearpaw and gives useful but by no means reliable support.

Snow-shoe types
The most common and popular snow-shoe on the market is the oval, almost egg-shaped Bearpaw, wide at the front, and flat, without an upturned toe. They start at 25 cm. (10 in.) wide at the

binding, and are a little over 60 cm. (24 in.) long. A snow-shoe of this size would give good support for a person of up to 63 kg. (140 lb.) in stable snow other than deep powder.

Add a pack and get the weight nearer 82 kg. (180 lb.) and the snow-shoe area must be increased to say 35 cm. (14 in.) wide and 75 cm. (30 in.) long. These basic Bearpaws are for trail work and backpacking in more open country.

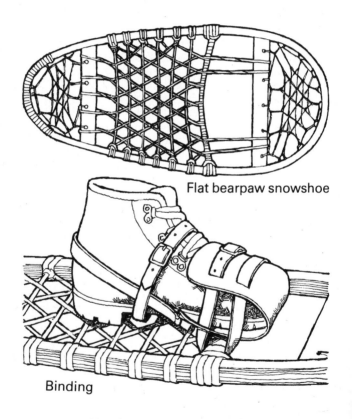

Flat bearpaw snowshoe

Binding

For forests or close country the best type is the Appalachian or Modified Bearpaw, which is longer, narrower and has a slight tilt to the tip. These are nearly all 25 cm. (10 in.) wide and up to 90 cm. (36 in.) long with a 5 cm. (2 in.) upturn and will support loaded backpackers up to say 90 kg. (200 lb.) on most types of snow.

Other snow-shoes are more distinctly shaped and have trailing tails. Snow-shoes are balanced *forward* so that this tail rests on the ground behind when the walker moves his or her foot forward, and acts as an aid to balance.

The popular model of this type is the Michigan, Maine or Beavertail snow-shoe, the type which most people visualise as a 'real' snow-shoe. These are of varying widths and lengths from 25 cm. wide by 90 cm. long (10 in. × 36 in.) up to 27 cm. wide by 137 cm. (11 in. × 54 in.). The former will support snow-shoers weighing about 49 kg. (110 lb.) and the latter snow-shoes weighing 107 kg. (240 lb.) including the pack. Other types, usually with Indian names like Huron, Ojibway or Yukon, are variations of this classic snow-shoe.

While rawhide is used for the classic webbing, most snow-shoes today have neoprene webbing, and leather strap bindings, which wrap over the boot and hold it to the snow-shoe.

Fitting

Snow-shoeing is warm work, but the feet can get chilled. The ideal snow-shoe boot is the Shoepak, mukluk type with a rubber sole and upper, but with breathable leather above the ankle. It is better if the boot has only a low heel, or a flat, built-up sole like a moon-boot. To fit the shoe, spread out the binding, with the long strap on the outside. Fit the boot into the binding so that the crossbar is in front of the boot and the toe end or bar is under the ball of the foot. Bindings vary, but the long heel-strap is a common feature and must be tight or the snow-shoe will fall off when walking. The toe of the boot will poke through the toe-hole between the toe-cord and the crossbar.

Crampons

Friction for walking or climbing is usually imparted by the webbing, but on crust or ice some sort of crampon may be necessary. It is often enough just to tie some knotted rope under the snow-shoe. Snow-shoe crampons are available, and the aluminium ones are light and easily carried and fitted.

Poles

Some snow-shoers manage without poles, but all concede that they are useful and occasionally essential. The ice axe fitted with a ski-basket is one good compromise, but two Nordic poles are even better. Poles do provide stability, especially when climbing, and must be recommended for touring.

Clothing

Snow-shoeing is not a rapid method of travel, merely a means of moving in deep snow. It is quite hard work and the rules therefore are the same as for Nordic skiing. Remove as much clothing as possible, move at a pace which minimises perspiration, and wrap up when you stop. The feet need special attention and must be kept warm. Beware of tight straps reducing circulation.

Technique

In the beginning, snow-shoeing can seem difficult. It is very easy to trip over the snow-shoes and hard to get up. Move slowly, resist the temptation to waddle like a duck, and lift the feet only enough to clear the other shoe. Otherwise you will develop crippling pains in the thighs and groin. In soft snow the shoe will sink in, and snow will gather on the top, adding extra weight, which has to be lifted with every step, so until your muscles get used to it, snow-shoeing is hard work.

Cultivate a gentle, flowing motion, allowing the weight to pass evenly from one foot to the other, and learn to pause between steps, relaxing the muscles. At the end of the stride the snow-shoe should be stamped lightly into the snow. This is useful in all snow states for it packs powder down and gives grip on crust or packed snow.

Reversing

The one thing you cannot do in snow-shoes is back up. The balance point sees to it that the tails dig in and any attempt to reverse will result in a fall. That apart, skiing techniques, like the kick-turn, are all possible in snow-shoes.

Climbing and descending
Climbing in snow-shoes is not easy and is usually achieved by traversing and step-kicking. The narrower shoes, at about 25 cm. wide (10 in.), can be edged in, but wider models just will not go in far enough to support the foot. If the snow is crusty it may be as well to take the snow-shoes off and walk up, kicking steps, or on crampons. The same holds good for the descent.

Breaking trail
Since touring, on both types of ski or snow-shoes, is hard work, it is as well to have only one track, and take it in turn to break the trail. Change places before the trail-breaker is exhausted. This could mean changing the leader every two or three minutes in heavy country. He or she simply pulls over and lets the next person lead through without stopping.

Winter travel
To sum up, the winter traveller needs to know how to handle at least one, and preferably two of these three pieces of equipment, to really get out into the snow-covered winter hills. Without such equipment and the techniques to employ it successfully, the winter traveller is confined to the lower slopes and to very restricted trips in shallow snow conditions. Once the snow gets much more than ankle deep, these are the tools to employ, and add the considerable joys of fast travel to the other pleasures of the winter world.

'Life is the art of drawing sufficient conclusions from insufficient premises.'

Samuel Butler

In the majority of cases the winter traveller will be able to shelter at night in accommodation not much different from that used in summer. In areas where ski-touring or hill walking is popular, the facilities are there to support it, and open to all. If the planned trip takes the traveller off the usual well travelled routes and into the back-country where he or she either has to, or prefers to, be self-sufficient, then there is always the winter tent.

Tents, though, even when effectively designed, do have operational limitations in winter, since it is almost impossible to keep them dry for any extended period. Spindrift will swirl through any gap, and even when it is very cold and perfectly dry outside, condensation inside the tent or ice on the outside will eventually dampen everything, and damp, as we already know, is the winter's most common threat. Alan Blackshaw took tents on his Scandinavian Traverse but told me that they very rarely used them preferring to shelter in huts, barns or snow-holes.

To some extent, the limiting factor in winter is how long you can stay dry or, once you get wet, on your ability to dry your clothing and equipment in the field, and so extend the trip. Tents will always be useful in winter, if only as a safety item, but to really live in the winter world you should be able to build your own shelter out there from snow.

Most experienced winter travellers will tell you that given the choice between a tent and a snow-hole, they will choose a snow-hole any time, if time and circumstances permit them to dig one.

Snow-holes are comfortable, draught-proof, easily lit, capable of enlargement at will, warmer and generally more fun. On the other hand, they take time and a little skill to construct, which demands tools, especially a shovel, and can be hard work. If you are on a tour and moving from point to point every day, then using existing huts, taking a tent or, better still, using a mixture of the two, is a more desirable option.

If you are in some fixed point for any period beyond one night, it is a better plan to dig a snow-hole, and enjoy the comfort and shelter that a well constructed snow-hole can provide.

However, we must take the broad view of winter and remember that it does not always mean snow. I am about to depart for the Alpes-Maritimes and today, in mid-January, there is still no snow along our planned route, so let us begin by looking at other forms of winter shelter. Some of these are often looked on as survival shelters, but this is just one application. If a shelter can keep you warm, comfortable and alive *in extremis*, it can do even better when things are going well. Besides, using such shelters as part of a normal outdoor routine is good practice against the evil day of disaster, should it ever come.

Some years ago, I met a party in the Auvergne province of Central France, who were staying in an hotel but going out each day on skis to build a shelter, here a lean-to, there a snow-hole, somewhere else a trench, even an igloo. This was done just for fun, but when they had constructed a series of shelters around the area, like spokes on a wheel, they went off in their second week on a circular tour and used these shelters as overnight stops. This seemed to me then an excellent idea, and I recommend it to you.

Lean-to's

Lean-to's can be constructed almost anywhere except on the bare treeless mountain, and the type you use depends on the materials available and the tools you have brought along, of which the most useful are a knife and a ball of string. Given time and environmental considerations, most lean-to's are a composite of natural materials and your own equipment, but this does not matter. The object is to construct a shelter which is adequately wind- and rain-proof, and good for an overnight stay.

For a simple lean-to, the first step is to find some natural windbreak, such as a low wall. If the wind cuts through the wall,

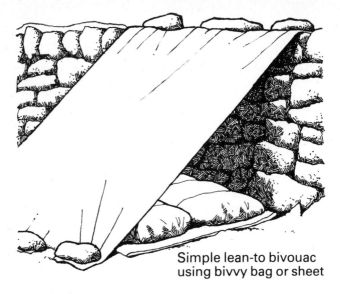

Simple lean-to bivouac
using bivvy bag or sheet

Basic brushwood
lean-to. Can be doubled.

chink the gaps on the windward side with mud or snow. You can then make a simple shelter with a bivvy bag, holding it to the top of the wall with heavy stones, and pegging it out at the bottom with stones, ice axe or ski poles, even just with packed snow. Then fill in one end of the shelter with snow or brushwood, lay out your windproofs for good ground cover, and settle in. It's not glamorous but it works, and if there are two of you in the party, as there should be in winter, you will have an adequate number of bivvy bags and cagoules for both ground cover and overhead protection.

In wooded country a lean-to can be swiftly constructed. Use standing trees or embedded branches for the uprights and lash a cross pole, even a ski pole, between the two. Then lean more branches against the cross pole, driving their bases into the ground. Roof this with grass, more branches, tree bark, your bivvy bags or even space blankets. Snow can be piled on top of this for extra insulation.

There are environmental problems here since it is bad form, or even illegal, to hack down branches from living trees. There is always enough dead or fallen timber around in winter to provide the bulk of the shelter, and your own equipment can bridge the gap.

An open lean-to of this type is not all that warm and really needs a fire in front to be fully effective. Here again, this is not a problem in wooded country, but remember the fire risk.

You can, of course, make a full-sized bivvy (or bivouac) which essentially consists of two such lean-to's placed together, rather like a grass hut. I have lived in one of these for a week in February on Dartmoor, and it worked very well. Put plenty of bracken or heather on the floor, cover the floor with a groundsheet and apart from some work filling in the gaps in the roof you will have a very workable shelter. These shelters may lack the snugness of a tent, but there is no condensation, and the problems of damp and rain coming in are little worse than you would find in a tent.

Snow-shelters
The essence of winter shelter, as you can see, is to let the countryside do most of the work. All you do is embellish or organise the existing cover into a passable shelter and settle in.

The same pattern holds good for snow shelters. Large natural objects like trees and rocks often offer the good beginnings of a snow shelter. With a fir tree you will have overhead cover from the branches, and if you work out from the shallow snow round the trunk you can soon construct a high banked area around the tree out of the wind. When the snow cover generally is inadequate you will find deeper snow drifted against walls, and this drift, and the wall itself, can be used to make a shelter. The traveller must use some imagination when looking at existing cover to visualise how that hollow in the rock, low wall or fallen tree could be transformed into a comfortable shelter, and for such purposes snow is ideal insulation.

Snow trenches
The simplest snow shelter of all is the snow trench. Digging down into snow is always possible, whatever the snow state, and a waist-high (or waist-deep) trench can be excavated by two people in

Dig out waist deep trench.
Pile snow around top of trench.
Roof with skis and ski poles.
Cover with bivvy bag and snow.

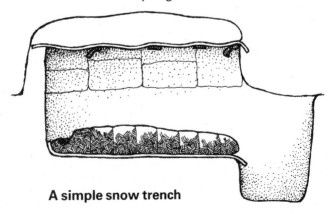

A simple snow trench

under an hour. As with all digging operations, remove as much clothing as possible before you start, to avoid it getting damp from sweat and melted snow.

Start by laying out and measuring the area to be excavated. I find that laying a ski on either side of the area gives a straight line and adequate headroom in the final trench. The trench can be dug out with ice axes and cooking pots, with the back of the skis, or better still with a shovel. Pile the exacavated snow around the top of the trench where it will freeze hard, and leave one of the narrow ends open, for getting in and out. The trench can then be roofed over with skis and ski poles, which are then covered with a bivvy bag, and held down with snow. Another bivvy bag goes in the bottom, but don't cover up *all* the bottom with the plastic bivvy bag. Leave a bare snow area at the open ventilated end for cooking in and taking off your boots. Snow on the ground bag will melt and soak your gear.

The trench walls can be excavated a little to provide niches for candles and by night-time you will have a very nice shelter, glowing in the dark. If it then snows, all well and good, for more snow on top is just additional insulation. Remember to have plenty of ventilation when cooking.

Snow mound caves
One of the problems when snow-holing is that there may not be enough good snow to make a proper snow-hole and snow, alas, can melt. Ideally, you need a good deep bank of firm snow, the type which can be hacked out in lumps, but if this bank or drift is not available naturally, then you will have to construct one.

The secret is to probe about until you find somewhere such as a hollow or a bank, where the cover, however thin, is thicker than elsewhere. This too follows the pattern of letting nature do the work.

Mark out a large circular area around the deeper patch, say 3 metres (10 ft) across or a little more. This is the ground area of your snow cave; place a ski pole firmly in the centre of this circle to act as an aiming mark. Now, mark out another area, another circle, around this first circle and at a fair distance away. The ring so formed should be at least as wide as the diameter of the inner circle at every point.

Then, starting at the *far side* of the outer circle, shovel or kick snow into the centre circle, aiming for the pole and piling the snow up into a mound around it.

The mistakes here are either not to have a wide enough outer circle and therefore end up with insufficient deep snow in the middle to make a cave in, or (and it's easily done) to start shovelling from the *inner* edge, and work backwards. This is not only hard extra work but results in a wide soggy ring around the central area across which the snow has to be transported. Always start at the outer edge of the outer circle and work towards the centre.

If you have done it right you will have a large waist-to-chest-high mound in the middle around the pole, which you shape roughly into a dome before standing back to await results. Put on a windproof and have a brew while the snow sets.

When snow crystals are rubbed together they melt from friction. The piled snow will quickly freeze solid, and you will be left with a

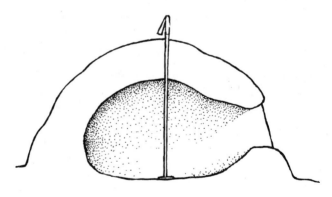

**Construction of a
snow mound cave.**
Pile the snow around ski pole,
tunnel in to pole.

deep mound of firm snow, ideal for tunnelling. Cut into this about a foot above ground level, and hollow out the centre until you reach the pole and then tunnel about until you have a decent sized cave.

I built two of these last year and they were quick to build, taking about an hour and a half from start to finish and gave very good, if cramped shelter. The only snag with a snow cave is that there is a limit to the amount you can tunnel in any direction without going through the walls. However, even a foot or so of packed snow keeps the wind out, and the more it snows once you are in, the better the cave becomes.

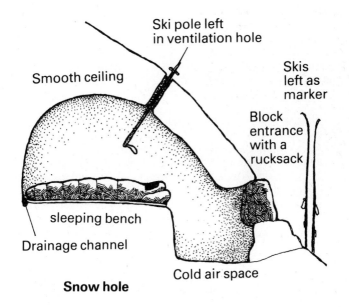

Ski pole left in ventilation hole

Smooth ceiling

Skis left as marker

Block entrance with a rucksack

sleeping bench

Drainage channel

Cold air space

Snow hole

Snow-holes

Most winter campers like snow-holes. They are not always joyous, and can become rapidly miserable if a sudden thaw sets in, but for the bulk of winter in the wild there are few things, outside a hostel, as comfortable as a well built snow-hole. If you have never built one, make a point of doing so this coming winter, and live in it for a few days. You will find that your snow-hole gets better every day and soon becomes a second home. A well built snow-hole can last several weeks and, indeed, a number of outdoor training establishments build some at the start of each winter so that if time and weather become problems their pupils can move in at once, without having to build their own.

Tools
You can build a snow-hole without any special equipment, using your ice axe for a pick, and your cookset lids as shovels. However, if you are going out with the intention, or possibility, of snow-holing, it makes very good sense to take (as a group item or one per pair) a snow shovel or a snow-shovel blade, of the type which clips on to an ice axe, and perhaps a snow-saw. These will make your task very much easier and save a lot of time.

Preparations
To dig a good snow-hole requires deep, firm, packed snow, and a safe location. Do not dig your snow-hole on an exposed slope or in an obvious avalanche slope or gully. Close under a cliff may result in a daily stone bombardment when the sun melts the ice above. Choose the lee side of the bank but don't go so close to the lee that your snow hole entrance is always drifting in. Move back a bit, to where the snow is packed firm. Find a site in an area of deep drifts with no obvious dangers, and prepare to settle in.

Probe the snow first with a reversed ski pole or the ice axe. You want to gauge both depth and consistency, and if the snow offers good but not iron resistance to your probe it is probably about right. If it comes away in good large dry lumps, so much the better.

Before starting to dig, remove as many clothes as possible and hand them to your companion. If he is not digging he can wear them to keep warm while awaiting his turn. Digging a snow-hole is hard work, and it is a good idea to share the work, changing over before one is too cold or the other too hot. On some occasions it is worth while digging two entrances to get into shelter quickly, after which the second entrance can be filled in.

Digging in

The entrance needs to be as small as possible in the end, but while digging in ignore this point and hack out a slot the size of the average door. This is extra work, but better and quicker than adopting a permanent crouch or burrowing like a mole.

1. To get the height, dig down, so that when you go in you are already in a knee-deep pit. It is much easier to fill in a gap at the bottom of the door than one at the top.

2. Go in about 60 cm. (2 ft) and then start to excavate the cave. It is important to establish the basic shape quickly, so that it is obvious to all the diggers, otherwise the hole will bulge in all manner of unnecessary directions.

3. Having gone in 60 cm. (2 ft) then start to clear away the floor area, working out in a full half-circle at knee height, and going back, say 90 cm. (3 ft). This area can be exavated up to head height. The snow can be shovelled or, if in blocks, manhandled out of the hole ready for future use.

4. At this point, your partner can move in and make himself useful, brewing tea, while you can proceed to excavate a wide sleeping bench at the back of the cave. Warm air rises and you will be warmer up on the bench, compared with down on the floor where the boots will churn up and melt the snow. Snow excavated here can be used to fill up the door space and the initial step until you have a level platform to the now much smaller door, and a wide sleeping bench above and behind it at the back of the hole. The sleeping bench may only have a marginal effect on warmth, but it adds greatly to comfort, and keeps the sleeping bag and mat away from crampon spikes.

5. Your basic snow-hole is now essentially finished, but can be almost continually improved. It does not matter if your snow-hole at present seems small, cramped, even

claustrophobic. Indeed, if it seems like this you have done well. It is a mistake to dig out more snow than you need to, for small holes are warmer than big ones; besides, improving the basic hole day by day is all part of the fun.

To get to this stage you will take about three hours, and as a rough guide you should allow one and a half hours digging for every member of the party and longer if you don't have a shovel. Smooth down the walls and ceiling to reduce the risk of melting snow dripping off the walls. Use a candle for internal illumination.

The entrance should be filled in until you have to crawl through it, but make it wide enough to take a rucksack without the sides crumbling. A rucksack can always be used to block the entrance at night, but always allow adequate ventilation, especially while cooking.

Snow-hole living

Here you are at last, in the hole, with night coming on and the keen wind howling outside. You now have to get organised.

One important point is to mark the location of the snow-hole, either by placing your skis and poles firmly at the entrance, or by putting up a stick with a coloured rag on top when you move out for the day. Snow covers up digging traces very quickly and your hole can be quite hard to find again without some kind of marker. Besides, it might stop someone falling through the roof, and giving all concerned a nasty surprise.

One basic task once the main shape of the hole has been established is to smooth down the walls and roof to eliminate sharp ridges. As the snow-hole warms up, any such surfaces will drip, so smooth the roof and walls carefully.

Ventilation

A ski pole should be poked through the roof and left there as a ventilation point, and to provide draught. With several people inside, a snow-hole will soon run out of fresh air, and the (very few) snow-hole accidents have nearly all been due to carelessness with stoves leading to carbon monoxide poisoning. Fill and light stoves outside, or at the step, just by the entrance – NEVER INSIDE. The thought of being trapped behind a wall of flame inside a snow-hole is appalling.

A burning stove eats up oxygen, so all vents, in door and roof, need to be open at this time, but adequate ventilation is needed all the time. If your candle (another oxygen consumer) starts to gutter or fails to burn, open up a vent. If you awake with a headache, or get one after cooking, these again could be signs that the ventilation is inadequate.

It is also necessary to keep the snow-hole cool, for if it gets warmer the drips and condensation are unavoidable.

Much of the comfort depends on the outside temperature which if below −10°C (14°F) will draw off excess internal warmth without trouble. If the outside temperature rises, the snow-hole may become untenable, so in such cases open all vents, cook outside and encourage the flow of cold air through the hole.

Organisation is the secret of snow-hole living, with a place for everything and everything in its place. Fortunately, snow is ideal for such a purpose. You can chop out shelves to hold kit or candles, and even one candle gives enough light to read by, for the light is reflected off the snow crystals.

Food keeps well if placed into a snow wall-cupboard, and everything can be emptied out of the sack and slotted into the walls. The only exception to this is the spare clothing, sleeping bags and boots which, when not in use, should be rolled up in stuff-sacks and kept in the rucksack.

When leaving the snow-hole for the day, or settling in for the night, always bring your digging tools, ice axe or shovel in and out with you. It may be necessary to dig yourself out in the morning, or back in again at night. When leaving the snow-hole for the day, cover it up by all means, but be sure to leave a marker on the entrance and be *very sure* you can find it again. Take adequate survival gear with you. Wandering the mountains at night, unable to find the shelter where you have left all the gear, could be alarming.

A two-man snow-hole will take around three hours to dig unless you are very experienced, and so if you are on a tour, digging one day after day is hardly practical. They are more useful as a site for a permanent base, which we can define as for two days or longer, or when your tent and other gear is so saturated that it cannot be used and your choice is either to come off the hill or settle in somewhere to light a fire and spend a day getting things dry.

Fires

As a rule, fires in winter are impracticable. They are never as good for cooking on as a good stove, and the environmentalists and most other open-air enthusiasts are dead set against them, so that on practical, moral and often legal grounds, fires are (forgive the pun) out.

Having established that, let me now say that there are circumstances where all the above can be forgotten and a fire becomes essential. If you are soaking wet and hypothermic, light a fire. If you must attract help, light a fire. If you need warmth, light a fire. None of these is a reason to set the woods alight, so, with fire, *be careful*.

Starting a fire

The secret of lighting a fire in winter is to start small. Begin by gathering all the wood you can, choosing dead branches, those sticking up in the air rather than wet fuel lying on the ground. Look in crevices and under rocks and tree roots for pine needles, dry moss and small dry twigs. You can also use your candle stub, wax scrapings, or fuel from your stove, this last being applied to the fire before you light the match or lighter. Warm a butane lighter inside your shirt pocket, and open up the jet for a full flame, before applying it to the tinder. As a bed for the fire use anything but bare snow. Lay out a bed of rocks or even wet branches, and put the dry fuel on top of them, otherwise melting snow will put the fire out.

Start with a small amount of tinder, about the size of your fist, and light it, just adding more fuel and longer sticks as the little fire gets going. You will need some sort of windbreak, so build a snow wall. You can break this down later when you need a draught. A stone base is useful under the fire, for the stones will get hot and retain warmth for quite a while. If you can build your fire close to a large rock, so much the better, for the rock will reflect the heat back out again.

Do not light your fire under trees, for the rising warmth will melt the snow of the branches above, and just when the fire is going nicely, splosh! down comes a branchful and puts it out.

When it comes to drying gear and clothes in this situation, dry the things that dry easiest and those which you need most. Dry the tent inner, your sleeping bag, and your socks, before worrying about the fly and any spare clothing. Dry your insoles, which you can dry in the open quickly, rather than your boots which take days to dry. Dry gloves are more important than a dry hat. Remember also to dry out the stuff-sacks which you keep these items in, or when you repack the dry items you will be right back where you started.

A good fire eats up fuel, so gather enough and more than enough before you light it and, as always in winter, be organised before you start.

Before leaving the fire, be sure that it is out. This may seem easy in winter, for all you need to extinguish a flame is to put snow on it, but fire can go underground, burning among the root systems for days and emerging elsewhere to start a forest fire.

Rake the fire apart, and put it out in detail, raking over the spot again and again until there is no smoke at all. Redistribute the ashes or wet base branches, and try to leave no trace of the fire, so that any heat patches will recover all the sooner. I cannot recommend fires, but if you must build one, then do the job properly.

Igloos
Finally, that most evocative of winter homes, the igloo. Hot from Canada, I learn that the word *igloo* is an Inuit or Eskimo word meaning home or shelter. It's always handy to speak a little Eskimo!

Ideally, igloos are constructed where the snow is dry (and therefore in sub-zero temperatures), and deep but flat. The Eskimo igloo is solid and windproof, but it does require skill to construct, especially in sub-arctic temperatures when the snow can be heavy and wet.

A two-man igloo needs to be about 3 metres (10 ft) in diameter and the process begins, as for the snow mound, by planting a centre pole – usually a ski pole – in the middle of the proposed floor area, and outlining a circle. The snow needs to be about 60 cm. (2 ft) deep and firmly packed. Cut out blocks of snow around the circle.

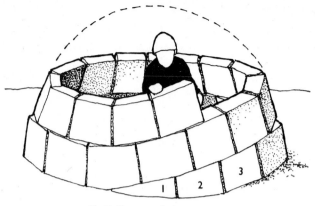

Building an igloo

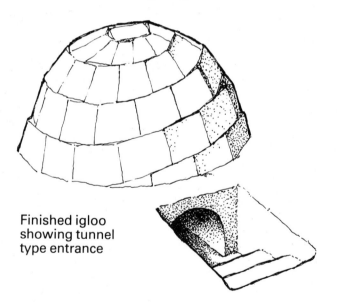

Finished igloo
showing tunnel
type entrance

They need to be 60 cm. (2 ft.) thick, or more if possible, and can be stacked around the circle rather like the base in a row of bricks. A snow saw is considered essential for cutting out snow blocks.

Continue cutting snow blocks from the floor in large manageable sizes, but as even and consistently as possible, moving into the centre and stacking the blocks higher, one on top of the other, around the walls, working in a circle and decreasing the radius by 15 cm. (6 in.) each time round.

Another recommended method of igloo construction is not to work in a circle, but in a spiral. The problem of igloo construction is to tighten the spiral so that the final block, or keystone, is reached before the walls fall in! Work from within, circling the walls and stacking the blocks up, chinking the gaps with snow.

In practice igloo building is much easier than it looks or sounds, because the snow block will freeze together and the bulk of an igloo's headroom is the result of excavation rather than wall height. A high, pointed igloo is a mistake, for any warmth will go straight to the roof.

You may run out of snow blocks inside the igloo, in which case an entrance must be cut in the walls, and more blocks passed through.

Once you reach the top, cut a large block to fill the final keystone slot. Fit this up from the inside and then chink it into position in the walls. This is best done from the inside, and if you have now walled yourself in and need an exit, just cut a small door through the wall, as low as possible and high enough to crawl through.

It is necessary, having dug out the inside of the igloo, to construct a sleeping platform. This is done by building a wall across the centre of the igloo and piling loose snow behind it. This will soon pack down and become firm enough to lie on. Loose snow may be thrown over the outside of the igloo to chink the gaps, and a low wall around the igloo on the windward side will help it to resist wind erosion.

From now on the igloo can be organised rather like the snow cave. To make the igloo, a shovel, firm snow and patience are essential, and you would be well advised to build one or two near home first, before relying on your ability to construct one in the wild.

Choice of shelter

The choice then for a winter shelter is between a lean-to, a snow trench, a snow mound, a snow-hole, and an igloo. The choice is dictated for you by the terrain, the snow, the availability of natural materials, and what tools you have with you, plus the usual abilities and techniques.

SHELTER OPTIONS

TERRAIN	SNOW STATE		
	DRY PACKED	POWDER	WET
DRIFTS	SNOW-HOLE	MOUND	SNOW-HOLE OR MOUND
DEEP BUT EVEN	TRENCH OR IGLOO	MOUND	IGLOO
SHALLOW	MOUND	MOUND	IGLOO OR LEAN-TO

Clearly the winter traveller will usually aim to stay in hostels or huts, or else carry a winter tent. Both save time, but there may be occasions when neither is available and it is necessary to construct a shelter from natural resources. The rule then is always to let the wild do most of the work.

These shelters are often presented as only feasible in a survival situation. They have, in fact, many more uses than that and the ability to construct adequate winter shelters is essential to anyone wishing to be considered competent in the winter wild.

Absence of body is better than presence of mind

Anon

At any time of the year a basic grasp of first aid is a useful outdoor skill. It may never be used for anything more serious than bandaging the odd cut or extracting a splinter, but such simple actions can make all the difference to the comfort of the injured person, and prevent an otherwise trivial situation becoming more serious. In winter, the very fact that the elements weigh in against the traveller means that slight injuries can have far-reaching effects, while the cold itself compounds all problems.

Prevention, as always, is better than any possible cure, so before reading this chapter go back and re-read Chapters 1 and 2, where the need for basic competence in understanding the weather and possessing and using the correct clothing and equipment properly is clearly stated.

Winter does have some advantages. The midge and black-fly have disappeared, and in the parts where they abide, bears and snakes are usually asleep. Heat stroke is less likely, and the use of skis can make long distances easier to cover without undue effort. So much for the good news, but to keep the account in balance, winter presents problems all her own.

Begin then by possessing, preferably personally but at least within the party, a sound knowledge of first-aid skills. Know how to bandage a cut, cover a blister, take a pulse. Know the 'recovery position', recognise when someone is ill or injured and know what to do about it, and on this foundation we can start to build an understanding of winter ailments and how to treat them.

Keeping the cold out
Cold is the main adversary in winter and must be combated with clothing, equipment and exercise. Keep active and you will keep warm.

Pay particular attention to the extremities: the head, the ears, the hands and feet. These areas are more open to the cold, and where the blood runs close to the skin's surface, as at the wrists and neck, it is more easily chilled, to the detriment of the whole body.

The head is like a thermostat control, so if you are cold put on your hat; if you are too hot take it off. Use the head to control body heat loss. Wear gloves, or better still mitts, and have a spare dry pair available. Gloves should have long cuffs to cover the veins on the wrists. Wear a face mask and goggles or glasses to protect the eyes and exposed skin from the glare of the sun and the effect of the wind.

Boots should be sealed against the wet with Nikwax or Sno-seal, and the socks changed regularly, for wet socks soften the skin, lead to blisters, and can contribute to frostbite. All these actions keep the cold out and provide your first defence against the worst of winter.

Stay dry

After cold the next enemy, and one which is more insidious and just as dangerous, is damp. Stay dry and you can resist a great deal of cold. Get wet and you will have problems, especially if the wind rises.

Early use of shell clothing will seal out exterior damp from most forms of precipitation, but do not forget the dampening effect of mist or white-outs. Wear garments made from snow-shedding materials, brush off any snow that falls on you, and knock the snow off branches and bushes before you push past them. Work hard to stay dry, but not so hard that you perspire, for this too is an insidious foe, equally damaging and harder to prevent. Use the clothing zips all the time to ventilate the body, and thermal underwear to draw perspiration away from the skin. Move slowly to reduce the sweating caused by physical effort, removing as much clothing as possible while on the move.

We have covered all these points before, but it is always worth remembering that in winter, especially, one action can initiate effects elsewhere, so never neglect to think.

Ski-ing in a snow storm

Fitness
To resist the sapping effects of cold and damp it pays to be fit when starting any winter trip. Tackling a trip for which the body is inadequately prepared can lead to all sorts of problems. It is essential before setting out in winter to be sure that everyone in the party is able to complete the longest possible day's stage, with full equipment. Trials may not be made over similar terrain, or on skis, but just realising how long the journey can be and how heavy a pack can become will concentrate minds most wonderfully and lead to sensible adjustments to equipment or routine.

Food and water
The next stop on the prevention road is to eat and drink adequately. A good breakfast to provide warmth and energy is essential, together with plenty of trail nibbles and, above all, lots of water. If possible drink warm water rather than that freshly unfrozen from the stream. Aim to eat around 5000 calories per day when on the move and as much water as you can drink, and you will avoid the problems of flagging energy and exhaustion on the trail.

Dehydration
My last action before setting off for a day out in winter is to drink plenty of water. Physical activity and dry air lead to rapid dehydration, and this in turn leads to early tiredness and headaches. Take in plenty of fluids, but avoid diuretic drinks like black coffee. The winter traveller will pass very little water, an indication of how much fluid is being lost by perspiration and dehydration, all of which must be replaced. A daily salt tablet will also help, but the basic remedy is a regular and plentiful intake of water.

First-aid kit
No well equipped outdoorsman or group travels without a first-aid kit, and the following items are the minimum it should contain:

1. Square of lint or gauze.
2. Roller bandages in various widths.
3. A tin of plasters, plus 'Moleskin' for blisters.

4. Several large plasters.
5. A roll of sticking plaster.
6. A fistful of cottonwool.
7. Three or four safety pins.
8. A tube of Savlon.
9. Some bicarbonate of soda and some salt tablets.
10. A small pair of scissors.

First-aid in winter

Giving first aid in winter is an action that requires some particular thought. Tightly bandaging a cut can contribute to frostbite in the limb. A casualty in shock or on a stretcher is particularly vulnerable to cold. All the basic first-aid routines, which all experienced outdoor people whould know – the treatment for shock, unconsciousness, severe bleeding – must be taken against a background overshadowed by the watchful menace of winter cold.

Medical aid

Do not consider your first-aid cover complete until it includes knowledge of mountain rescue posts, doctors, hospitals and police. Medical aid can be required for a wider range of problems in winter and you must know where to find it.

Sunscreens

To the basic three-season first-aid kit the winter traveller must add a heavy lip salve, and some face cream. Chapped skin and split lips are not fatal but they are not much fun either, and all too common in winter.

Glacier cream is very effective, as is the thicker white zinc-oxide sunscreen. Pay particular attention to lips, nose, forehead, and the area under the chin and behind the ears. Sunlight reflected from snow gets into the strangest places and can cause uncomfortable burns.

Heat exhaustion

Man is a homothermic creature, that is, a creature which needs to keep the body temperature within very strict limits, at about 37°C

(98.4°F). Variations of even half a degree can cause those aches and pains which everyone has experienced at the onset of a cold. The dangers of hypothermia, or loss of core heat, have been frequently and wisely aired, but it is a fact that far more people die annually from the opposite condition, heat exhaustion.

Heat exhaustion is rarer in winter because the air is usually dry and the body can dispel excess heat by sweating. However, the traveller can induce heat exhaustion in winter by sealing off the body in shell clothing so that perspiration and body heat cannot evaporate, while the body is continually losing salt. The body's central heat mechanism can then fail and collapse is inevitable. It is necessary to strip off the clothing to let the body breathe and, if the casualty is conscious, to give salt in solution. Airing the body, drinking lots of water, and taking a daily salt tablet are the best preventive measures.

Hypothermia

Hypothermia is a loss of body core temperature, the core consisting of the vital organs of the body; heart, lungs, liver and brain. As we have noted earlier, the body can lose heat in a number of ways, by radiation, evaporation, condensation and convection. All such loss can lead or contribute towards the state of hypothermia or exposure.

The causes of hypothermia

Apart from carelessness and faulty technique on the part of the victim, hypothermia is caused by:

1. Cold, but not necessarily sub-zero temperatures.
2. Damp, by precipitation, perspiration or immersion.
3. Wind and the windchill factor.
4. Exhaustion.
5. Any combination of the above.

Exhaustion is often due to the victim undertaking a trip beyond his or her physical prowess, or simply not being fit enough or well enough equipped to fight the effects of the weather, or failing to take in sufficient calories to maintain the needed energy level.

Symptoms
If the body core heat is lost or significantly reduced, the victim
becomes increasingly ill, a state which begins quite slowly with
shivering and slurred speech, and then rapidly develops into
stumbling, falling over, irrational behaviour, unconsciousness, and
death. Hypothermia develops fairly slowly, but once the initial
symptoms appear more severe ones quickly follow, so that, as
always, prevention is the best solution.

In winter the body draws most of its warmth from the calorific
value of food, so that good food and plenty of it are the best
defences against hypothermia. Then, to defend the body against the
elements, the right clothing is essential. Even this may not be
sufficient if the causes of hypothermia act in combination, and good
technique is required to combat this winter killer.

Treatment
Early recognition of the symptoms is essential, and the feature that
may first draw attention is uncharacteristic behaviour, verbal or
physical. Sudden chatter, singing, being argumentative over small
points, stumbling on the trail or falling over, all may indicate the
first signs of hypothermia. If you 'wonder what's up with Jim this
morning', wonder again if it might be hypothermia, and act. Do not
wait until the victim collapses.

Treatment consists of two steps:

1. Prevent further heat loss.
2. Re-warm the victim.

If you are close to a suitable base, return there at once and place
the victim in a warm bath or shower. That would be nice and
convenient, but it is rarely practical. People have been struck down
by hypothermia just after returning to base, so if you are shivering
in the hut and unable to get warm, then consider the possibility of
hypothermia and act.

Out on the hill, the first action is to stop and get the victim out of
the wind. Pitch the tent if necessary, and get the victim inside. Strip
off any wet clothing, and replace it with plenty of dry garments.

Place the victim in a sleeping bag, and put someone else in for extra warmth, for the hypothermia victim cannot generate heat of his own. This second member should strip down to the underclothing to provide direct body heat. It may be possible to light a fire, but in any event do not forget ground insulation for the victim and the possibility that if one person has got clear symptoms of hypothermia and has collapsed, other members of the party may be very close to it, particularly if they are now standing about in the cold. Everyone should put on warm clothing, get into a lee, and start to brew up.

If, and only if, the victim is conscious, give him a hot drink with extra sugar. Boiled sweets or glucose tablets are also helpful, but alcohol is harmful and should never be given to hypothermia victims. Do not force fluids into unconscious persons, for they cannot swallow and may choke.

If the victim is unconscious, he should be placed in the 'recovery position' in shelter and on adequate ground insulation, not on bare snow or frozen ground. Send for help and continue the re-warming process until help arrives or the victim recovers.

When the victim recovers, do not at once proceed on your way. It is necessary for the victim to have a complete rest, and it is best to pitch camp and wait a clear day before proceeding. If shelter is close at hand the victim should be carried there, however much he or she protests and claims to be all right. Rest and food are necessary to restore the victim before any further effort is attempted, and this must be supplied and its beneficial results clearly seen before the recovery can be said to be complete.

It should not be thought that hypothermia only occurs in the sub-zero mountains. Walkers at sea level, even dinghy sailors, are at risk from hypothermia, and people have been struck by hypothermia when the air temperature was well above freezing.

Hypothermia is much more common among outdoor people than they themselves often realise. Who has not found himself unable to stop shivering, or spent much of the night curled up in a normally adequate bag, unable to get warm? Mostly we are lucky, and recover from the mild effects with rest, food and warmth, without noticing them very much.

If matters had gone just a little differently, though, the condition might have developed to a serious degree, so it pays to think about hypothermia when the weather is foul, and take steps to prevent it developing in the first place.

Frost nip

True frostbite is mercifully rare in the British hills, but by no means unknown. Modern equipment and, I like to think, a growing competence among outdoor people has led to a decline in the number of victims, even though more and more people are going into the winter hills. Frost nip, though, is still quite common, and while fairly mild, it is still an irritating condition and one which can be easily prevented.

Frost nip is a severe chilling of the flesh, the ears, nose, feet or fingers, which usually occurs in windchill conditions, and may not be noticed at the time. The true effects are seen later, when the skin cracks and weeps, opening into purple sores or cuts which are slow to heal.

It can be noticed by the occurrence of white patches on the skin, or a numbness in the finger tips. When this is noticed the affected part should be covered up and re-warmed. A handkerchief tied across the nose, or a band round the ears held in place by goggles, is usually adequate. Chilled fingers can be placed in the armpit or mouth and re-warmed. As warmth revives the affected area it will sting a little, but if this done early enough no damage will result. It is, however, a feature of frostbite injuries that a part once affected is prone to fresh attacks. My ear-lobes were once severely frost nipped and still crack open very quickly if I forget to cover them. Wearing a hat in cold weather is therefore a sensible basic precaution.

The treatment for frost nip, then, is prevention, identification, and re-warming.

Frostbite

True frostbite is much more serious. It will cause severe pain, and it can lead to tissue loss and the amputation of limbs. Moreover, like hypothermia, it is often the cumulative result of a number of contributing causes, and therefore insidious. On the other hand, it can usually be prevented and, when detected, simply overcome in most outdoor situations. There is nothing inevitable about frostbite, and people have come down off Everest after a night in appalling weather with all their fingers and toes intact. They knew what to do, and did it, and so must you.

Causes of frostbite
Frostbite commonly occurs in the body's extremities, in the ears, fingers, toes, hands and feet. Hypothermia is one cause of frostbite, for when the body's core heat starts to fail, warm blood is transferred from the extremities to the core, thus robbing the limbs of vital warmth, and laying them open to frostbite.

Windchill can freeze the face and fingers, especially if the victim is already damp from perspiration. Contact with cold objects can cause frostbite, since the chilled metal will suck warmth from the skin very quickly. If the feet are chilled and lose feeling, watch out, and as a first precaution remove those chill metal crampons from the boots.

Spilling petrol on the skin is very dangerous at low temperatures and very easy to do. The fuel bottle usually stays in the fly at night and the contents will be super-cool by dawn. Finding the stove empty for the morning brew, you then spill petrol over your hands. Petrol evaporates from the skin quickly, increasing heat loss, and as this petrol will be well below zero, your flesh will freeze. Use a funnel or, better still, fill the stove carefully the night before. The obvious solution of keeping the petrol bottle in the tent is not such a good solution when you take into account the other facts of night-life under canvas, such as cigarettes and candles.

Shock after injury may cause frostbite, and casualties have been frostbitten while being carried out on stretchers. The rescuers, with much to think about, forget how cold the victim can get. Always cover a stretcher case with a rug or sleeping bag, and remember to keep him or her warm.

Dampness, the old enemy, can add frostbite to its long list of resulting ills. Wet feet lose warmth and freeze easily. I believe that wet feet in winter are inevitable, and as long as they are wet *and warm* it hardly matters, but if they are wet and cold or, worse, start to lose all feeling, then it is time to stop and chafe the feet back to warmth. Flicking them with a towel is very effective. Once they are warm put on dry socks, and dry the boots out with a towel.

Frostbite is a freezing of the tissues and this can be due to heat loss from all the causes we have already examined.

Beards do not cause frostbite, but they make the detection of frostbite symptoms more difficult, and by accumulating snow and ice beards can help to freeze the skin underneath.

All these factors, separately or in combination, can cause frostbite.

Symptoms
A chilling sensation is the first sign, followed by a loss of feeling in the affected areas and the appearance of white patches on any exposed skin. The skin and, in severe cases, the flesh, feels hard. Blisters may appear on the skin later. Frostbite symptoms may not appear on the trail but may manifest themselves at night, when the injured area is re-warmed, when it can swell, throb and become extremely painful. If the frostbite is deep, the pain will be severe enough to prevent further travel, and medical assistance is vital.

First aid for frostbite
Firstly, appreciate that frostbite is very serious. The experienced traveller should never allow the symptoms to develop past the frost-nip stage without taking action. This action *never* involves rubbing the affected part with snow, which is a dangerous myth. The first aid for frostbite is the same as for frost nip.

The numb area must be re-warmed as quickly and gently as possible. Fingers can be re-warmed in the mouth, and the ears and nose can be covered. Remove crampons and boots and place the feet inside the shirt and against the body of a trail-mate. This is when you find out who your *real* friends are! It is important to re-warm the affected part *completely*, for partial re-warming and then re-freezing does great damage.

Only the most superficial frostbite can be treated on the trail. If the casualty is badly frostbitten it is much better to walk out on frozen feet to medical aid rather than re-warm feet on the trail, for it will be impossible to walk on frostbitten feet after they have been re-warmed.

Clearly, a doctor needs to be consulted, but if one is not available or cannot be quickly consulted once shelter is reached, then the injured part can be re-warmed by placing it in a warm bath, with the temperature a little over 37°C (100°F). Medical assistance is still necessary, and the risk of gangrene, infection through frostbite sores, and tissue loss is very high.

The first-aid treatment for frostbite is therefore as follows: If you can, prevent it; if you suspect it at an early stage, re-warm the affected part; if it is severe, get the casualty to medical help.

Snow-blindness

The sun's glare, reflected off the snow, is the principal cause of snow-blindness. The eyes become inflamed and feel gritty and if the situation goes unchecked it may lead to temporary blindness.

Wearing sunglasses or, better still, snow goggles which fit close to the eyes and exclude the glare, is the best preventive action. If the ailment develops, cold compresses will help, as will wearing dark glasses. Wet, cold tea-bags are said to be good. Aspirin will reduce the pain and eyedrops will help to control the inflammation and the unpleasant 'gritty' feeling. Treated in this way the problem should clear up in two or three days.

Mountain sickness

Whenever someone ascends rapidly to a point significantly higher than the area in which they normally live, the body suffers from oxygen starvation. This can occur throughout the year, but is more often encountered in winter when skiers climb high to start a ski tour.

For walkers and skiers the effects are usually fairly mild, but as I am a sufferer I can vouch for the fact that the effects are unpleasant, even in the milder form. The effects are noticed at about 1800 metres or more; breathlessness, headaches, inability to sleep and depression.

The answer is acclimatisation, but this takes time, so it helps to combat the effects as they arise by taking it easy for the first day or so, taking aspirin for the headaches and a small sleeping tablet to get to sleep for the first night or two, and realising that the misery you feel is more imagined than real.

There are those who cannot cope with mountain sickness and have to come down again, but at the heights reached by the bulk of walkers and skiers mountain sickness may not occur at all, and anyway it will soon disappear as the traveller becomes acclimatised.

Carbon monoxide and anoxia
Winter being what it is, there is a natural tendency at night to close the hut doors, zip up the tent flaps and get a good fug going. This can have dire results. Cooking produces carbon monoxide, and a very small amount of this in the air can produce unconsciousness and death. Carbon monoxide is a colourless and odourless gas, and since it is always present when cooking on petrol stoves be sure to ventilate well and preferably cook in the open, or with the door wide open. Tests have established that much less carbon monoxide is produced from petrol stoves is produced from petrol stoves if the cooking flame is clear of the bottom of the pot, for carbon monoxide is the result of incomplete combustion. The rule remains though: ventilate well when cooking.

Anoxia simply means '*lack of oxygen*', and while less lethal than carbon-monoxide poisoning is still unpleasant and sometimes fatal.

A cramped hut or tent full of breathing bodies and without ventilation will quickly run out of oxygen. Dim or guttering candles are one obvious sign, and the result is that you wake up in the morning with a foul mouth and a headache. Adequate ventilation especially when cooking, is the best answer, but remember that anoxia can lead to death.

Winter, as you can see, compounds three-season ailments, and has particular problems all its own. The winter traveller must know first aid, be aware of the problems caused by cold, wet and windchill, and know how to combat them. In winter, prevention is always much, much better than any possible cure.

'The beginning of wisdom is a salutary shock'

Arnold Toynbee

Throughout this book I have tried to avoid making continual references to 'survival' and 'danger'. Personally, I feel that most books and articles on outdoor activities in winter tend to labour 'survival' to the extent that after you have read a number of them you start to feel insecure in your own back garden unless equipped with ice axe, crampons and a rucksack full of mint-cake. The basics of winter survival are contained in the Mountain Code listed in the appendices.

The underlying fact of winter out of doors is that while most of the 'risks' are the same as in summer, the margins of safety have been reduced. That minor sprain or compass miscalculation which causes a small problem in summer may, but only may, lead to a survival situation in winter. For this reason, people going any distance out into the winter wild should:

1. Have some three-season experience.
2. Plan their trip properly.
3. Carry a reasonable amount of equipment.

If everyone did that then survival situations would not arise, except for that very rare event, the unavoidable accident. The medical hazards of winter were discussed in the last chapter, but here we are concerned with the elements. It is useful to remember that a hazard can be induced by an attitude or action and is not necessarily inherent in the situation itself.

In this chapter we shall look at the specific hazards of winter and what to do about them, concluding with a short section on survival. To the extent that the book is about living and travelling outdoors in winter, the entire book is about survival, but the word 'survival' has its own precise definition: *'to come through alive'*. We will examine winter travelling in the light of that definition, with the addendum that the aim is to come through comfortably and happily as well.

Many winter hazards are avoidable, but one, the weather, has inevitably to be faced.

Severe weather

Winter weather of the severer kind, combining, as it can, cold, rain and wind, inevitably saps the strength of the traveller. It needs good equipment, care, and technique to combat the effects of a winter storm, and the best technique is adequate preparation.

A good grasp of weather lore is essential, but it is essentially worth remembering the effect of altitude on winter weather in the hills. Going from 500 m. (1640 ft) up to say 1800 m. (5900 ft) you will inevitably meet a severe drop in temperature, often exacerbated by the stronger winds common on exposed slopes. Quite apart from the increased exposure on bare slopes or above tree level, the temperature 'lapse rate' ensures that temperature falls about 3°C (5°F approx.) with every 300 m. (980 ft) climbed. You must dress suitably for the heights you will travel at, not for the valley floor, a fact which is frequently overlooked in the late spring or autumn. Cold, and especially cold compounded by wind, is the cause of many problems (see Wind chill chart, page 20, 21).

Rapid changes in weather are another feature of winter. Conditions may change from calm to gale in a few minutes, and it is necessary to carry a range of clothing suitable for a wide variety of weather conditions.

Lightning is sometimes a feature of winter storms and is by no means only a summer phenomenon. It is thought to be connected with cloud temperatures below freezing, and will strike most often on the heights. If ice axes or metal objects start to 'buzz' get off the heights quickly and cover metal objects.

Darkness

Winter days are short and can be made even shorter by overcast skies and lowering cloud. Even on days when darkness is supposed to fall at, say, 1700 hrs, it may be too dark for safe travel by 1530 hrs. Darkness imposes all sorts of restraints. It may be impossible to find waymarks, or read the map and compass, and being benighted on the trail without sufficient equipment for the night can be unpleasant. Always aim to be inside your shelter one hour before dark. A torch is essential, as are spare batteries and bulbs.

Mist and fog

Mist and fog are two major winter problems. Visibility tends to be restricted in winter anyway, and this naturally causes navigation problems against which the first and best defence is good map-and-compass skills.

Accurate compass bearings are often more useful than a map in poor visibility, and the taking of back-bearings is always advisable. Maps should be on a large scale, say 1:25000 certainly in the hills and must be continually consulted and used in conjunction with the compass, for in close visibility the traveller will have to proceed in short bounds from one identifiable object to the next. Never miss a chance to take a bearing or fix your position in winter, for mist can close in with great speed. Always know where you are.

Mist and fog have a considerable dampening effect on clothing, and freezing fog is a menace, coating rocks with ice. Crampons may be needed on narrow paths in fog, even where there is no obvious snow or ice cover.

White-outs

A white-out occurs when fog or cloud cover descends over snow. The light is flat, there are no shadows, snow and sky merge and travelling in such conditions is slow and hazardous. Quite apart from the risk of a fall over a bank or into an unseen crevasse, navigation is difficult in white-outs, since it is hard to see which way you are going, and all too easy to veer off course.

Throwing snowballs ahead of you to see where they land is one method of testing the lie of the land, and if the snow is crusty you can usually tell if the slope is leading you up or down, by sensing the slope through the soles of your feet. If you are on a marked path, follow it carefully and watch for cairns, stopping if one fails to appear, and casting about until you find it.

You can also proceed on compass bearings, sending one person out ahead to the limit of visibility, and one behind moving him right or left on to the bearing, while the whole party keeps moving, which is quite accurate, but slow.

Coming down off the hill can also be hazardous in poor visibility or white-outs. It is easy to neglect proper navigation and get careless on the way down, especially when tired or feeling that the trip is practically over. Keep to proper procedures and don't get careless. Following streams as an obvious route can lead you over sharp drops, since water takes the shortest route off the hill. It is always advisable to stick to defined routes and move slowly. Contouring slopes is very difficult in poor visibility, for it is difficult not to lose height or direction, especially when moving on skis and constant use of the compass is essential.

The greatest comfort when travelling in poor visibility is to be certain, from previous study of the map, that you know the lie of the land and with good map and compass technique can maintain your direction, and know at all times where you are. Use the map and what it tells you to stay away from cliffs and ridges in poor visibility.

Ice

Ice (verglas) is a definite winter hazard. It is pretty to look at and can provide drinking water, but by and large the disadvantages of ice outweigh the benefits. Ice on the hills or slopes must be countered with ice axe and crampons. Boots alone are rarely adequate.

Ice-covered rivers may and sometimes do provide an easy route across difficult terrain, but even in North America and those parts of Europe where rivers freeze inches thick for months on end, ice travel must be viewed cautiously. In Europe river ice is rarely thick enough to give reliable support and the best advice for Europe is to stay off river ice entirely, although well frozen Scottish lochs, make for fast travel – provided the ice is reliable.

In North America, where walking the river ice is accepted, there are still some rules to follow:

1. Stay away from projecting rocks and tree trunks, since the ice is thinner there.
2. Where rivers join, get up on to the bank. The turbulence of the water will mean thin ice.
3. If a stream joins the river from one side, walk on the opposite side, or go on to the bank.
4. Walk on clear ice rather than on snow-covered ice.
5. Carry a long pole for testing the ice, or to span the gap should you fall through.

Streams

Crossing unfrozen streams is also hazardous. The rocks will be slippery and may well have an invisible ice coating. The risks of getting soaked by a fall in winter should make you hesitate, for a soaking in below-zero temperatures can be serious.

Move upstream until the stream is bridged or can be jumped, remembering that overhanging snow banks may provide a poor foothold for take-off or landing, and make the stream appear much narrower than it really is. One tip for crossing mountain rivers in winter, if you must, is to do so early in the morning, when the night-time freeze will have reduced the flow. I have seen a raging afternoon torrent reduced to a trickle by morning, only to rise again as the sun warmed the air during the day.

Snow

The winter traveller will meet all types of snow. It looks pretty, but it can cause hazards. Keep falling snow out of your packs and clothing. Do not let it accumulate and melt on your clothing. 'Anti-glis' snow-shedding clothing is useful here. Snow can obliterate tracks and will conceal cairns and markers, and slow your progress considerably, so if it starts to snow, think of the hazards that could occur and act to thwart them. If you have not already done so, take a few bearings and fix your position on the map. Think about the distance you plan to cover, and close the party up. Put on windproofs, and press ahead to get into shelter as soon as possible in case the snowfall turns into a blizzard.

Blizzards

If the snow arrives driven before the wind, a blizzard may develop, and blizzards are by no means an arctic or mountain phenomenon. Indeed, the worst blizzard I have ever encountered was on the South Downs of Sussex, in the South of England. It is essential to seek shelter, dropping into the valley, getting into a lee, retreating to a hut, or pitching camp to wait out the storm.

Cornices

Cornices are caused by the wind. This drives snow over the lip of ridges and gradually moulds it into an overhang. Cornices can be very thick and are virtually undetectable when approached from the windward slope. Walkers frequently walk up quite unknowingly on to cornices to admire the view or check their location, quite unaware that they are out beyond the edge of the ridge and standing on unsupported snow.

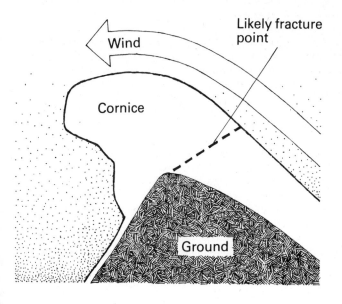

Moreover, should a cornice fracture either through its own weight, a change in temperature, or the weight of a walker or climber, it will fracture at an angle well behind the actual edge of the cliff it overhangs. Walkers should assume that any snow-covered ridge is to some extent corniced, and stay well below the apparent crest.

Crevasses

Moving on after a heavy snowstorm can be hazardous. The snow is often soft, deep, unstable and prone to avalanche. New snow may well conceal crevasses, particularly in glaciated country. In summer most glaciers are 'dry', that is to say, they are clear of snow at least along the lower stretches, when they resemble nothing so much as dull grey jumbled mazes. In winter they look like rivers of snow and are very beautiful, but the snow usually varies in thickness and will conceal many rifts, or crevasses. Crevasses are by no means confined to glaciers and can be found in any snowfield; crevasse rescue techniques can be used to extricate travellers from any hole into which they have tumbled.

Crevasse rescue requires a rope and some knowledge of ropework. The process adopted will depend to a very large extent on whether the casualty (a word I shall use here to describe the person in the crevasse) was roped up or not when he or she fell in. Travellers crossing a glacier should certainly be roped up against just such an eventuality and possess prussik loops, or even jumar clamps for use in the event of a fall.

The snow which covers crevasses is often thick enough to provide a snow bridge if the gap is narrow, but no one should attempt to cross such a bridge without being roped up. Concave, sagging, snow-bridges should always be avoided. It may even be possible to climb down into the crevasse, step across the gap and climb up the far side. A rope is a necessary group item when crossing snowfields or glacier country, and the pre-trip study of the map will reveal whether such terrain lies on the route.

If the party does not have a rope and someone falls into a crevasse then they have a serious problem and must send for help.

Crevasse rescue

A party crossing a glacier or snowfield should be well separated and roped up. Note the following points:

The usual rope is 9-mm. nylon Kernmantel, and this comes in 45-m. (150-ft) lengths. The party should rope up, with the leader and the end man using a bowline with a stopper knot and the middle men using either the alpine butterfly or the middleman's knot. For the purposes of this book I will assume a party of four, one of them a 'casualty'.

The leader and end man should not tie on to the exact end of the rope but leave themselves some few feet of spare rope for use in case of emergency. There should be about 10 m. (30 ft) of rope between each member, allowing the end man some 10 m. (30 ft) of spare rope which he can carry in a coil. Thus organised the group may proceed.

It is essential to move slowly in such country, the leader studying the surface and probing ahead. If he goes through the surface the rest of the party should plant their ice axes fast and deep into the snow, and lie on them. The ice axes will act as a belay, and the fall will be arrested, hopefully before the leader has gone down too far. It sounds simple, but it doesn't always work out like that. When we were practising this in the Cairngorms, using a low cliff as our 'crevasse', the student leader slid gingerly over the edge, there was a 'twang', and the second man shot over after him! The third, who had seen it all before, planted his axe and held both of them until we all stopped laughing, and started to discuss how we could get *two* people back up again.

The first step is to arrest the fall. When it is clear that the rope is adequately belayed by at least one and preferably two members, the last man goes to find out what is happening to the casualty.

Hanging down, full weight, in a loop of rope, will certainly be uncomfortable. The casualty's first task, if conscious and in a position to help himself, is to put a loop in the spare length of rope and get his foot in it to relieve the pressure on his chest or abdomen. Having checked that the casualty is conscious, not in a panic and able to assist, the survivors' next job is to check the belays.

Assuming for the purposes of this example that the leader has

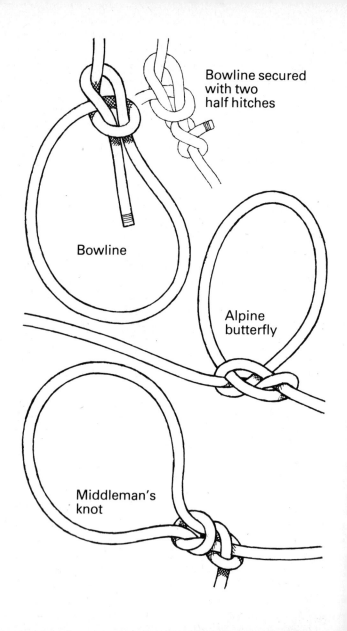

Bowline secured with two half hitches

Bowline

Alpine butterfly

Middleman's knot

Party roped with ice axe in right hand and coils in left

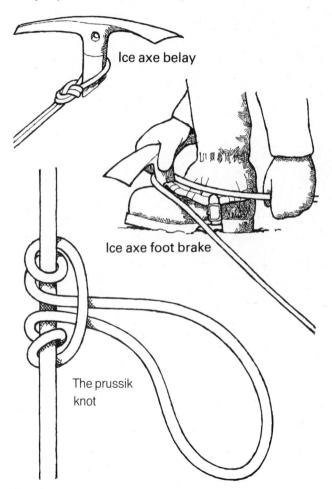

Ice axe belay

Ice axe foot brake

The prussik knot

gone down, the second man stays in the snow as a firm anchor, while the third man should plant his axe very securely and belay the rope to it before untying himself. Ice-axe shafts are not designed for this and must be placed deeply to be effective. This gives a situation where there is a casualty in the crevasse and one man is belaying the rope, with two axes serving as extra 'deadmen', and two men now available with about 30 m. (100 ft) of rope to help the casualty out of the crevasse. Without prussiking, the casualty will probably not be able to shin up the rope from his end, and prussiking requires a sling on the rope *and* knowledge of the prussik knot.

The two on the surface can either tie foot-loops in their end of the rope and lower it to the casualty, so that he can climb out using it while they assist him by taking up the slack on the main rope, or they can make another bowline in their end and attempt to haul him up on that. It may be necessary, if the casualty is injured or unconscious, for someone to descend into the crevasse to help him.

If the casualty was not tied on when he or she fell into the crevasse, or was wearing skis, the problems are greater, and indeed the whole area of crevasse rescue is very 'iffy'. The weighted main rope will cut deeply into the snow at the edge of the crevasse, making it hard to haul on. Some recommend that a rucksack or bivvy bag be placed under it to prevent it cutting deeper, but no one can explain how you take the strain while this is done. However, putting a bivvy bag under the lowered end is obviously a good idea.

Usually the casualty sinks in rather than falls, and is able to get some support from the walls, particulary if the crevasse is narrow and he is wearing crampons. If it is possible to lower him down on to a ledge so much the better, as this will give everyone time to think, while easing the strain on the casualty's chest or waist.

Crevasse rescue is a fairly advanced technique and one which, like ice-axe work, must be learned and practised by the group as a winter skill. It is often taught using special crevasse-rescue or climbing equipment, such as prussik loops or metal jumars. The average winter traveller will not have such equipment or be able to use it. It is worth mentioning that even experienced mountaineers rarely need to employ crevasse-rescue techniques, but it is necessary to have at least an outline plan for action in the event of a crevasse accident.

Winter travellers, then, when travelling across potentially hazardous or crevassed ground should:

1. Equip the party with 45 m. (150 ft) of Kernmantel rope and prussik loops.
2. Practise crevasse rescue drills.
3. Rope up as described.
4. Proceed with care, testing the ground, and only crossing snow bridges in cases of dire necessity.

In the vent of a fall, avoid panic, and:

5. Check the state of the casualty.
6. Ease rope pressure on the casualty's body by using a foot-loop or lowering him to a ledge.
7. Belay the rope to prevent further fall.
8. Prepare a rescue plan as outlined above.
9. Put it into effect and rescue the casualty.
10. Re-group, sort out rope, rope up, proceed.

This is a highly specialised topic, and I recommend a close study of 'Modern Snow and Ice Techniques' by Bill March (Cicerone Press, 1973).

Roped skiing
The above procedure assumes that the party is on foot. On skis, the party can still rope up and proceed as described, cautiously and as well spread out as the rope permits. Roped skiing is not difficult providing the members of the party control their speed and close up to provide slack rope for the turns, although only snow-plough or gentle stem turns are really possible when roped.

If someone goes through into a crevasse, the whole party should fall over and jam their skis into the snow at right angles to the tautening rope, which is the natural reaction anyway.

From then on the drill is as described above, coping with the necessary steps as quickly as the equipment permits. Practice is obviously advisable.

Avalanches

Avalanches are a winter killer and all winter travellers must beware
of them. I have before me a thick pile of press cuttings recording
avalanche injuries and deaths during the last two winters and they
record a catholic range of victims. Walkers, climbers, downhill
skiers, cross-country skiers, motorists, people in hotel rooms or in
their gardens, guided parties and lone skiers, amateurs and experts.
Avalanches are striking people down all over the world in spite of a
great increase in avalanche know-how, mammoth investment in
avalanche protection, and pre-emptive action by avalanche patrols.
Many of these deaths are due to the fact that there has been a great
increase in winter outdoor activities, and since this book will
contribute to that growth it seems both fair and wise to include a
section on avalanches, their causes and how to avoid them.

My first recommendation is that all winter activists, whatever
their particular bent, should read Colin Fraser's *Avalanches and
Snow Safety* (1978) published by John Murray, London. This was
originally published as *The Avalanche Enigma* and is available in
various languages as the definitive work on this fascinating subject.
I have listed it in the bibliography but I want to stress its importance
here and declare that, as essential reading, you should obtain a copy
and study it thoroughly. Apart from being authoritative it is very
well written and by no means heavy going.

The second point that has to be made about avalanches is that
they can happen anywhere and kill anybody. An avalanche outside
Lewes in Sussex in the South of England in 1836 demolished a
number of houses and killed eight people. There is a pub on the site
today called the Snowdrop Inn, and the inn sign records this unusual
tragedy. Only two years ago an avalanche killed Dougal Haston, an
Everest mountaineer of high repute, while he was skiing just behind
his home in Leysin, Switzerland. It happened to him and it can
happen to you.

Clearly then, expertise and experience will not help you if an
avalanche strikes, so the rule must be to avoid them whenever
possible. To achieve this end the traveller requires a thorough
knowledge of snow.

Snow states

Snow mechanics is a complicated subject, but the winter traveller needs to have some idea of what happens to snow after it falls, how it reaches a 'trigger' state, and how it is set to avalanche.

Falling snow lands in many states, from feather-light and dry to wet and heavy, depending on the air temperature. A heavy snowfall lasting several hours can contain various layers of snow, from wet to powder dry, and this fact alone is a potential source of trouble. Once the snow lands it starts to compact and change and begins a process known as *metamorphism*. This falls into three broad stages, called *destructive*, *constructive* and *melt*.

The *destructive* stage involves the rounding down of the individual sharp snow crystals, and the creation of water vapour by pressure between the crystals and the various snow layers. During this process the snow will compact and settle as the air is extruded, and the snow height will reduce. The higher the temperature (and the temperature often rises after a snowfall) the quicker this process will be and the more marked the effect. Under stable conditions a fresh fall of snow will complete the process of *destructive metamorphism* in about three days.

The second phase is *constructive metamorphism*. This, too, is caused by temperature changes and moisture between the snow layers. It will be colder on the surface where the snow is exposed to the air, and becomes warmer as the layers get deeper, although the temperature is always below freezing. The layers gradually fuse together, extruding water vapour, and the crystals increase in size as the vapour rises through the layers towards the surface. The result of this process is the creation of large crystals, up to half an inch long, with a depression at one end, and for this reason called *cup crystals*. These crystals are angular and do not fuse easily with the other, smaller, crystals. An unstable layer is therefore created in the snow, and the formation of these crystals marks a major step towards a trigger state.

Melt metamorphism is the melting and refreezing of the upper layers as a result of air-temperature changes, and ends up producing snow crust or ice.

One final result of the metamorphism process is the production of *surface hoar*. This is caused when extruded water vapour reaches the surface of the snow and meets the colder air. This hoar will produce crust, and if fresh snow falls on top of it the result is yet another unstable layer, and yet another trigger mechanism.

The result of all this is that snow layers are inherently unstable and often contain layers of cup crystals and surface hoar as prime trigger points.

Snow is both viscous and elastic. It will tend to flow, yet is cohesive and elastic enough to hold together for quite a while even when unsupported. This too is a matter of common observation, for snow can be seen overhanging any roof eve, and will often stay there for days before falling or melting away. This gradual overhanging action is called *creep*, and it is worth noting, for snow will 'creep' on any slope until it eventually reaches break point and comes away. Creeping produces tensions within the snow, and can trigger avalanches on both concave and convex slopes, although convex slopes are marginally more risky than concave ones.

The causes of avalanches

Snow is inherently unstable, especially after the processes of metamorphism, but metamorphism is not in itself a cause of avalanches. Most avalanches have to be triggered.

During a snowfall the amount and nature of the snow deposited may be critical, and a snowfall in excess of, say, 30 cm (12 in) will create an avalanche risk, particularly if it falls in a blizzard and is wind-driven into drifts over a short period of time. The state of the previous snow layer is also important. New snow on surface hoar may avalanche, and the very weight of the new layers may be enough to set the cup crystals rolling under the previous metamorphised snow cover.

Terrain is also a factor, although it must be remembered that small avalanches occurring on 15° slopes have killed people after flowing only a few score metres.

However, the majority of avalanches occur on slopes of over 25°, and most of them on gradients of between 30° and 50°. Above 50° the slopes are too steep to allow enough snow to gather, and below 30° avalanches are slow and shallow. These comments are necessarily general and should not lull the reader into thinking that if the party stays off slopes of between 30° to 50° all will be well.

An avalanche could begin high on a mountain on a 40° slope and plunge, gaining momentum, down a 50° slope to sweep across a 15° slope or even a flat valley and engulf you on the far side, and it is safe to say that *any* slope can avalanche.

Altitude seems to have little direct effect on avalanches, for while there is usually more snow the higher you go, the steeper slopes and exposure to wind above the tree-line mean that generally the snow has less chance to accumulate to a critical point.

Normal ground cover is also a factor. Deforestation has exposed the lower slopes to avalanches, but while travelling in woods is generally safer, avalanches have destroyed woods without undue trouble. Gullies make natural avalanche chutes and should be avoided, particularly if corniced or after a snowfall.

However, the fact is that all snow is inherently unstable and becomes more so as metamorphism takes place, so that outside factors simply influence an existing situation.

Skiers have triggered avalanches by crossing unstable snow. Climbers have dislodged cornices which have disturbed snow on the slopes below. Noise itself is not a major factor, so whispering your way across tricky slopes will not help if the snow is due to release. Avalanche patrols use the concussion of dynamite explosions or even shell avalanche slopes with field guns to dislodge avalanches, but in these cases it is the vibration rather than the noise with sets the snow in motion.

Other factors which have influenced the start of avalanches are more easily identified. A fresh snowfall can add just enough extra weight to start a slide. Rain-storms and rising temperatures can increase the weight of existing cover and provide water to lubricate the slide, and such wet snow avalanches are especially lethal because of their crushing weight and the fact that when they eventually halt they quickly freeze solid, entombing anyone trapped under the surface. I have myself been knocked down by a small wet snow avalanche and had to be hacked free with boots and a shovel.

As you can see, practically any factor, or combination of factors, can start a snow slide. Only experience, judgement and great care

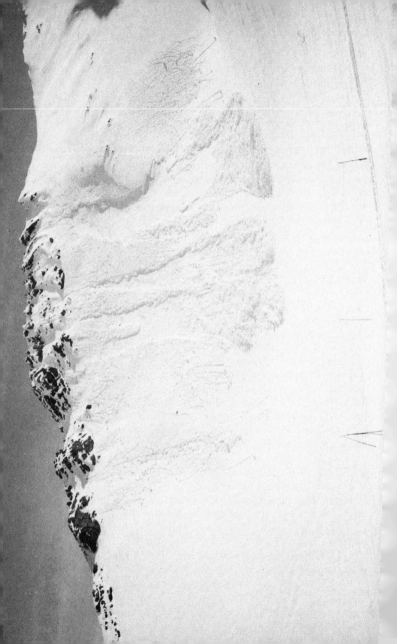

can warn the traveller when any slope is critical and best avoided. This experience is provided in most areas by Ski or Avalanche Patrols, by Park Rangers, and by the local people who know their area well. Ignoring their advice or pre-avalanche warnings can be fatal and is the mark of a fool.

Types of avalanche

The winter traveller will soon start to notice avalanche paths in the mountains. He will see the long smears of raw snow down the side of slopes and ridges and hear the boom and rumble of falling snow and rock. These avalanche paths repay study, for they can show where avalanches occur locally, and how far they travel. After a while such study induces an awareness of critical areas, and you will thereby learn to avoid them. There are two main types of avalanche, the *slab* and the *loose snow*, the first visible as a wide fracture, the latter a spreading smear from a single point high on the slope.

Slab avalanches can be either broad or narrow and often occur when frozen slabs break loose from the packed snow, and slip away down the slope. This often occurs after blizzards when the wind has packed the snow into precarious places from which, when the wind stops and the temperature rises, it easily breaks away. These are basically dry slab avalanches, and they are often found on lee slopes where the snow has packed down out of the wind. Beware of such dry slab avalanches below cornices or running down gullies after a blizzard.

Warm weather is the main cause of wet slab avalanches. We saw a lot of these in the mountains of the Picos de Europa in Western Spain, where the Atlantic winds dampen the snow. These are thick heavy avalanches, which may start slowly and heavily but leave a high deposit of huge snowballs and frozen snow when they eventually stop. Their weight alone can make them lethal.

Loose snow avalanches are even less predictable. The most destructive form of avalanche is the *airborne powder* type, which can work up to tremendous speeds, travel for miles and do immense damage.

Avalanche trails

Large or small dry, loose snow avalanches can be seen everywhere in the mountains. They start at a single point and widen as they travel, forming a broad arrowhead pointing up the mountain.

Wet, loose snow avalanches have the same shape and, being heavier, are slower than the dry snow type, but much more dangerous. People have been killed by wet snow avalanches because they seemed to be slow-moving and therefore harmless. Skiers have stopped to watch the avalanche flow towards them, and have then been knocked down by the weight and buried. When this avalanche stops the snow will set like cement, and by no means all wet-snow avalanches are small. If they start on a steep enough slope and gain momentum, they can build up speed, weight and power.

While these are the main avalanche types, any one avalanche can contain several types, one triggered by another. I have, from time to time, been asked to describe the drill for surviving an avalanche, and I have always declined to do so, for the best way to survive an avalanche is to avoid it by staying out of danger areas, particularly if avalanche warnings have been posted. I do not subscribe to the opinion that avalanches are an acceptable risk which an experienced outdoorsman can survive, if he knows some suitable 'technique'. There are some steps you can take if caught in an avalanche, but it all happens so fast that it takes a very quick-thinking person to apply them, although I do know two people who have used them and survived. Both avalanches occurred in the UK and were started by people above them dislodging snow on cornices. The first sustained multiple injuries, including a fractured spine, the second got the fright of his life and was dug out bright blue. Both were 'experienced' outdoorsmen, but neither is keen to repeat that particular experience. However, for the record, here is what to do . . .

If you are avalanched

1. Be aware of the risk at all times: carry a sonde and cross exposed slopes singly, with wrists out of the ski-pole loops, and pack harness loose.

2. If the avalanche has caught you or is about to, get rid of skis, poles and pack. The torque on these caused by moving snow can and will cause multiple fractures to your limbs.
3. Try 'swimming' with arms and legs, doing the backstroke, in an attempt to stay on or near the surface. Rolling hard, to stay at the front of the slide, is also worth trying, and perhaps more natural.
4. Keep your mouth shut, and as the slide slows, try to clear the snow away from your chest and mouth, to provide a breathing space. Try and create air space, for you will need it.
5. If you are trapped under the snow, try and fight free before the snow sets. Let saliva run out of your mouth and see which way it runs, to avoid digging down, rather than up.
6. Try to remain calm. Shouting is of little use, for snow deadens sound, and while the victim may hear his rescuers they will be unable to hear him.

Avalanche equipment

The first useful device is the avalanche or *oertal* cord, 50 to 60 metres of red perlon line marked with small metal arrows. The traveller ties the cord around his waist and trails it behind him. In the event of an avalanche knock-down this line tends to flow up to the surface, where the rescuers can follow the direction arrows and uncover the victim.

The avalanche cord works, but it has to be said that even when people take them along, they usually remain in their pack. These cords should be tied to the waist and used. They only cost about £4 ($8), weigh very little and can often be hired.

Technology has also moved in, with the introduction of the 'sonde', a radio transmitter popular with ski patrols and mountain rescue teams. The two main systems are the *Pieps* and the *Skadi*. The *Pieps 2*, which is the most common sonde available in Europe, is made in Austria, and has a transmitter and receiver button. When setting out the skier switches to *send*, and if he goes under the rest of the party switch to *receive*, and search in the direction of a loud regular *bleep*. Even deeply buried casualties have been picked up from 30 m. (100 ft) away.

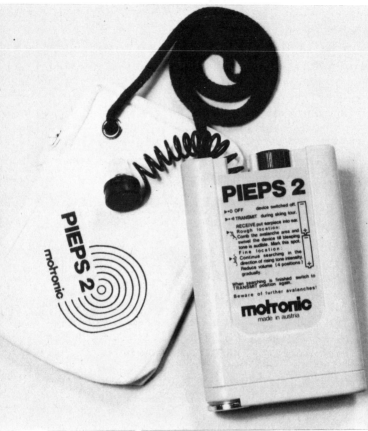

The Pieps 2 – a transmitter/receiver

The snag with such transmitters is the cost, but they can be hired from outdoor shops, and I would regard them as essential stores for ski-mountaineering parties. They are used extensively by Park Rangers, ski instructors and Mountain Rescue teams. If they find them useful the less experienced should find them essential.

Avalanche rescue

If a slope avalanches with your friend on it, do not scream, shut your eyes or look away. Watch what happens and mark the spot where your friend disappears. The search will start between the point and the end of the avalanche.

Speed is the essence of avalanche rescue, so as soon as the slide stops, start an immediate search of the slope. With upturned ski poles probe any dark spot or around any abandoned gear. If the victim was using an oertal cord, this may or should be on the surface and can be followed to locate the survivor. If there are any other parties in the area enlist their aid, but if the first rapid search reveals nothing you must send for avalanche teams equipped with probes and dogs. A sonde can save life here.

While this is being done the remainder of the party can go over the slope again, 'rough-sounding' with their ski poles. This is more effective if it is done by a properly organised search-line rather than by a group of dazed, shocked skiers probing about aimlessly. If the pole strikes something solid, use the shovel to dig down to it. Finally, while searching the slope, be aware of the risk from further avalanches. It is perfectly possible for a slope to avalanche twice, and the second slide can be even more devastating than the first.

Clearly, the basic advice is to heed avalanche warnings and stay out of avalanche areas at high risk times, for once the avalanche has struck someone down, their chances of survival are slim.

This 'winter hazards' chapter has covered most of the major problems that can affect travellers in winter. Most of them are avoidable, with a modicum of care, and the pure 'accident' is very rare. The bulk of accidents are caused by inadequate preparation, poor equipment and carelessness.

Most accident victims make some significant contribution towards the problem, and have only themselves to blame when things go wrong. If you plan ahead, act sensibly, and work as a team, you will have very little trouble.

Planning

It would be unwise to leave this chapter without stressing some points which we have covered elsewhere. In winter it is essential to plan. Just going out into the hills won't do. You must collect relevant information and apply it, make your plan and stick to it; but sticking to the plan is only admirable if the plan, in the light of events and in the conditions of time and place, turns out to be feasible. Plan escape routes and don't be too proud to take them.

Survival
If you are in a survival situation all the information in this book, if applied, will be useful. Make for shelter if you can. Look after the injured or weaker members. Act as a team and as friends. Think!

1. Find a natural lee, like a low wall or a wood.
2. Otherwise excavate a small snow-hole, or dig a trench.
3. Put on warm and shell clothing, covering in particular head and hands.
4. Huddle together for warmth, sitting on anything other than the snow or bare ground.
5. Put the feet inside rucksacks, hands into armpits or groin.
6. Get into your bivvy bags.
7. Prepare a brew, eat some chocolate or high calorie food.
8. Keep stamping and slapping, or do isometric exercises to keep warm. Check the state of your colleagues.
9. Don't worry.
10. Sing, chat, tell stories. Wait.

Like this you will survive even the worst of winter rages for a fair while and maintain your ability to do more if the weather worsens, or be fit enough to move on if it abates.

Remember that in survival situations snow is your ally. If it is still snowing after an hour or two, the material to make a shelter lies all about you, or is packed up into a drift behind a wall. Winter is only an enemy if you think of it as one.

'There is little point in setting out for a place one is almost certain to reach'

H. W. (Bill) Tilman

The time has come to put all this into effect and go somewhere, so when the leaf turns, look to your maps. Out of doors, winter arrives early. The wise traveller forgets the calendar and ignores the shopping-days-to-Christmas yardstick, for these are simply man-made calculations, and lack all power to instruct the elements.

Effectively, winter begins in October and lasts until early May. During that period the traveller in the hills goes equipped for winter conditions, and should be prepared to cope with snow.

Having said that, I have to point out that I have just descended from the hills high above St. Martin Vésubie in the Alpes-Maritimes of France, where there was no snow at all. I walked without a shirt on, and one of the mountains was ablaze with the first forest fire of the year. The month is January.

However, this very day and not a hundred miles away to the west, in Languedoc, the Army and helicopters have been called in to help villages cut off by blizzards. In winter unreliable weather can always be relied on.

There is, of course, no real need to spend the winter on long ski trips, or in hand-to-hand combat with the elements. Move to warmer climes, stay out of the hills, and your winter trips need involve little more than the effort to cope with rain and mud. That is possible, but rather dull, and the best weapon against a dull trip at any time is to start with a good idea.

Ideas
Most winter trips really begin when somebody gets a good idea. The idea may be sparked off by almost anything, a summer trip, a film

on television, an article in a magazine, even a postcard, by anything that can plant the seed which says 'That would be somewhere to go, or something to do, in winter'. To process this idea from an idle thought into a viable plan can be a long and (for me, anyway) enjoyable process and one which must start with a decision on three basic points:

1. The object.
2. The group.
3. The time.

Winter trips must be planned. There can be no question of just shouldering your pack and heading off into the hills. Try that and you won't go far, or very often; the weather will see to it that sooner or later you will come a cropper. All good trips will have an object and must be planned in order that the object is achieved: so, clearly, defining the object is both the first step of the plan and a major one towards achieving it.

On other than day trips you need companions. The received doctrine says that the ideal number for an extended winter trip is four. I have often gone with just one companion, but except on trips across populated terrain I have never gone alone. In winter, solitary travel is not sensible, or very much fun, and I prefer to have a companion. On the other hand, group trips present problems of time, organisation and, not least, compatibility. If the members don't get on, or one member regards the rest as coolies, a group trip can be misery.

Finally, you need a sensible timetable, out and back. Time is money and neither is usually in inexhaustible supply.

Once the objective has been agreed on, the problems thrown up in selecting the group and fixing the time requirements have a habit of falling into place.

Winter trips, as we know, must be planned and a good plan depends on accurate information, of which more anon. The first step is to have a broad outline of the idea. Do you wish to travel

Map reading on the trail

from home or from a fixed base elsewhere? At home or abroad? In the hills, mountains or flatlands? On snow or off? By ski, and if so which type; on snow-shoes or on foot? Will you stay in huts, backpack, or do only day trips?

These can only be outline preferences but they are worth recording before you get the group together and start to assemble information a task which is quicker if shared, and more effective if the results are checked by others.

The group
The idea usually starts with one person, who, while the plan is being formulated, will round up a group of like-minded friends. A group is necessary for any decent trip, so there is little point in discussing the merits of group versus individual travel.

The leader – and the leader may be defined for my purpose as the person with the original idea – is the organiser, or motivator, and usually the one who selects the group.

The most important group quality is compatibility. Nothing is more miserable in winter than sharing a hut, tent or snow-hole, with constant bickering and tension in the air. It's supposed to be fun, after all.

Individual skills can vary immensely, and should add to the collective strength of the group. A good navigator, a good cook, someone with relevant languages, and someone who knows the terrain and has skills to cope with it could all be useful. Opinions outside the event in hand, on religion or politics or what you will, do not matter, but outdoor attitudes must be about the same. It is worth checking, though, that someone with relevant skills is willing to use them. When one of our party lost an argument with a wall, our medical member handed me the first-aid kit and said 'You do it, I'm on holiday'.

The outline plan will influence the leader in choosing his or her group and in selecting people who would like to do the trip and are *collectively* up to the challenge. Individual skills can vary, but there must also be group ability at a common level.

Ski-mountaineering in the Swiss Alps

As a basic standard *for the group*, all members should have the necessary equipment, be fit, and have adequate ability in the basic skills. It is pointless enlisting a non-skier for a ski-mountaineering trip, or planning a long ski tour with people who have no idea of Nordic technique. Expertise may not be needed, but basic competence is essential, and a short outing with new people to check they can do all they claim is a worthwhile precaution.

At this time, with an outline plan and an interested group, the organiser should get agreement on the trip itself. The object needs to be agreed, and the various means of achieving it decided upon. Routes, daily stages and allocation of equipment can be thoroughly discussed, not just because decisions on such points are useful in themselves but because this discussion will reveal latent incompatibilities. If three members agree on a hut-to-hut tour on cross-country skis, while the fourth declares that *he* will take snow-shoes and camp out because that is what *he* wants to do, then he should be dropped. Agree the end and the means, and then divide up the tasks necessary to get the project under way.

Information

A plan is only as good as the information it is based upon, and in winter, make no mistake about it, a good trip needs a good plan.

Your plan must be based on information which is:

1. Up-to-date.
2. Relevant.
3. Reliable.

The only way to ensure this is by checking, re-checking and counter-checking, for people will offer as immutable facts information which turns out in practice to be completely inaccurate.

Having done all that, the wise winter traveller hedges his bets and allows for the fact that, plan as you will, something will go wrong. Given that a group has been formed and the objective agreed, the leader can delegate the collection of information among the members, reminding them that good information is vital and no unchecked information reliable. This will not only help the group to pull together, it will give the less experienced members some idea of what they are up against, out in the wild.

It must be appreciated that very little if any of the available information will have been collected with your trip in mind. You have your own group and particular objective and must piece together the information you require from bits and pieces produced for other reasons, or for a different purpose entirely.

The information requested depends on the trip, but the following headings will serve as a basic list.

1. Weather, snow cover, avalanche problems.
2. Terrain, maps, guides.
3. Accommodation – refuges, huts, campsites?
4. Transport in, out and over.
5. Equipment, personal requirements, group requirements.
6. Food sources and supply. Shops?
7. Trails available, waymarking?
8. Emergency cover, rescue services, doctors, insurance?

This list could be extended almost indefinitely, but will serve as an example.

Weather
The weather is clearly the main factor. Will there definitely be snow cover? Is there a history of storms? Is the weather cold but reliable, or cold but unstable? Declaring the object of the trip to informants is essential if you are to obtain reliable information, and weather centres at least are staffed by scientists who will provide accurate information even if the weather is the most problematic area of all.

Terrain
Terrain can often be judged from the maps. It is necessary to obtain maps of at least 1:50,000 scale, or better still 1:25,000 or the equivalent, and if possible obtain them at home. It may be possible to work out the route from large-scale maps, but if you rely on obtaining 1:50,000 maps in some mountain village you may be disappointed. It is a fact of outdoor life anywhere in the world that

the local maps are always out of stock. If good maps are not available at home then it may be necessary to divert through a large city to pick up maps on your way to the start. Foreign maps may differ significantly from O.S. maps and repay a little study before use. The best map and guide source in the U.K. is Stanfords Map Centre, 12 Long Acre, London WC2. The Royal Geographical Society, Kensington Gore, London SW7 2AR is another fruitful source, as is the Map Library at the British Museum. Other countries have their own topographical surveys and produce more or less accurate maps to various scales.

More information on the terrain can come from a number of sources, and apart from the obvious sources of information – guide books, holiday tour brochures – even postcards or photographs can give valuable information. All visual information is especially useful.

Accommodation

Accommodation requires considerable consideration. The ideal winter tour is one which uses huts, tents and snow-holes as the situation requires. Quite often, a lack of information – no open huts, insufficient snow for snow-holing – throws the traveller into taking tents as the only reliable option. Accurate information here is clearly vital to avoid taking excess gear or setting out inadequately equipped.

Transport

Transport services in winter are often meagre or irregular, a factor of particular note in hill country where even summer services are usually inadequate. Airports can be fogbound, trains and ferries delayed by frozen points and gales.

Check timings, and allow for delays. A tight time-schedule which depends on public transport will almost certainly go wrong. If you are travelling to the starting point by car, the car itself needs to be winterised, and equipped with a roof-rack, snow chains, plenty of anti-freeze and a well-charged battery.

Winter walking in French Pyrénées

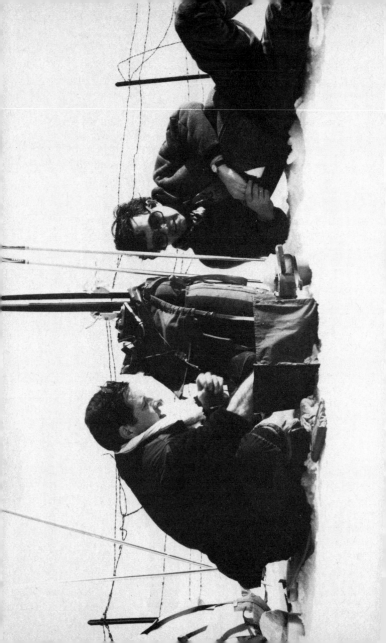

Equipment

A *complete* list of equipment should be prepared for each individual and for the group. See Appendix 1. Extra items may need to be acquired, and certain items like ski-bindings and crampons need careful fitting. All this must be done at home and checked carefully. Some items, like ice axes and crampons, can be hired, but hire items must be carefully checked for wear. I prefer to have my own equipment, or borrow it from a reliable friend, so that at least I know who has handled it before. All kit should be cleaned, checked and tested before you leave.

Food

Food is a problem, for you need plenty of it and it can be bulky and heavy. Personally, in spite of the cost, I tend to use A.F.D. (Accelerated Freeze Dried) foods in winter, from such firms as Mountain House, Springlow or Raven. For savings in weight and convenience of cooking they are worth the price, although they need to be balanced with some fresh foods where available.

On longer trips it may, even so, be impossible to carry all the necessary food in the group's rucksacks, which leaves the members with the choice of:

1. Replenishment.
2. Caches.
3. Sledges.

Replenishment points – small villages or other places where shops are open – may be located on the map, but this depends on the food shops being open in winter, which is by no means always the case.

Caches are useful, especially as freeze-dried food is rarely available in normal shops. Caches can be established by post, sending parcels 'post-restante'. Small hotels, Youth Hostels, Park Rangers and the like will readily accept parcels and hold them for your arrival, and even alert the rescue services if you announce you are coming and fail to arrive.

A short brew-up stop on the Traversée du Jura

Caches in the wild are more difficult to establish, and to find again, but they can be set up from the car if you are using transport and points on your planned route are accessible by road. If there is a road, though, there are usually villages for replenishment. Animals, notably mice, will quickly locate food supplies and spoil what they fail to consume, so any cache should be in a sealed tin, either buried under rocks, or hung up out of reach. Mark the site so that the group can find it, but not so obviously that passing thieves or vandals are able to remove it.

Water may also be a problem, and water supply points should be noted. You can usually melt snow, but it uses a lot of fuel. And then there is fuel . . . the list is endless.

Sledges
One option which is popular in North America and Scandinavia is the use of sledges. Even a light sledge can transport a great deal of food, but the techniques of sledge handling over varied terrain are not learned in a day, nor are sledges everywhere available. Sledges remain an option and one which is well worth considering for extended trips in remote terrain, but their use and handling takes practice.

The one-man cross-country sled

Trails

Even in very remote country, some trails may be available and they can be very useful in winter either as clearly defined routes to follow or as checkpoints along the way. Waymarked summer footpaths are often used for winter ski-trails, and usually lead to reliable accommodation. However, it is necessary to check if the trail is waymarked for winter. Paint marks splashed on rocks now under snow are not much help. Cairns and high finger-post waymarks are much more reliable but, however good the waymarking, never neglect to use the map and compass. Waymarking always peters out at just the wrong moment. On the relative values of map and compass opinions seem to vary. I have read books by quite eminent outdoor people who decry the use of the compass in winter and claim to work off the map. Personally, I use the map as a check, and run in the main on compass bearings, from one point to the next. It never occurred to me to do otherwise, especially in the poor visibility common in the European winters. Sensible use of both map and compass is the wisest course.

Emergency cover

The winter group should be self-sufficient and able to cope with any foreseeable emergency. To be prepared for unforeseen emergencies and accidents you must know, and have marked on the maps, all huts and rescue centres, and likely sources of telephones, doctors and hospitals. This is fixed information, very easy to acquire, and you will feel very foolish if, after an accident, you rush to some village which has no telephone, or spend hours fruitlessly hunting for aid. Know where to get help, and hope you will never need it.

Insurance

Insurance is also important and you should, as for any other holiday or trip, never leave home without having adequate and unequivocal insurance cover.

This list of information can be expanded almost indefinitely. It depends on the trip, and the object you have in mind, but all information is useful, and it is far better to have too much than not enough.

Detailed information is essential and the traveller must never forget the little points. Everyone remembers the big issues, but the little points are vital. Can you get gaz cartridges locally? Are the hostels open? Yes, but in *winter*? Are you sure? Be wary of vague replies 'It *should* be all right . . .' 'I believe so . . .' 'Probably. . . .'

You need to *know*, and even so, have a little something in reserve for *when* (not *if*) the information you've been given lets you down.

Sources of information

Once you have decided on what you need to know, the likely sources of information will probably occur to you, particularly if you ask yourself who is likely to need this information in the normal course of events. Typical sources include:

1. Embassies and Consulates.
2. National and Regional Tourist Offices.
3. Meteorological Offices.
4. Alpine or ski clubs at home and abroad.
5. Walking or footpath organisations.
6. Tour operators.
7. Outdoor magazines.
8. Members of previous expeditions.
9. Libraries.
10. Airlines.

A letter published in an outdoor magazine will usually provoke a response, and the more detailed the letter the more reliable the reply.

Reconnaissance

If you want something done, do it yourself. The ideal way of collecting information which is up to date and reliable is to make a pre-trip reconnaissance, either the same winter, or the winter before, or in the previous summer. In this way you can see the terrain for yourself, collect accurate information and make friends, even establish caches, and, in short, do anything and everything necessary to ensure that the plan works.

A reconnaissance is not always possible but it is always advisable, and if it can be done, then do it. Failing that, a long detailed chat with someone who knows the area well is almost as good.

Alternative plan
One wise option, well worth including at the planning stage, is that of the alternative plan. Winter is fickle, and it is impossible to say exactly what will or will not be possible when the starting date arrives.

An alternative plan gives the group the chance to divert from the main objective on to some other one, and should enable most of the pre-trip plan to be put to use. It need not be inferior to or easier than the original scheme, but it should offer some clear alternative if, for any reason, the first idea proves impracticable.

Fitness and trial run
Keeping fit in winter is always a problem. Particularly if the time available is short, there is always pressure to bite off more than you can chew and then overdo it. To be enjoyable the trip must be within predetermined physical limits, and these should be tested.

A short excursion before the main event is always a good idea. Even a day, or even better, a weekend trip, will shake the group into a team, show up any inadequacies in equipment and give you some idea of whether the trip itself is feasible. If not, there is still time for some final adjustments before the big day arrives.

Getting there
Getting to the starting point is all too often a frustrating experience, and is usually accomplished in something of a rush. Try and be absolutely ready at least two days ahead, all packed with nothing to worry about but the weather and nothing to do but check forecasts.

Kit lists are essential tools and all items should be checked into and out of the transport at every stage. In the excitement it is easy to leave behind equipment that cannot be easily replaced. Nothing is more frustrating than to arrive at the start without your ski boots, for example.

If travelling by car, check everything into the car, and be sure that roof-rack items are secure and well stowed. Skis should be bagged against grit and road spray, or they will not take wax.

Cars entering mountain territory should be equipped with snow tyres or chains, and carry a shovel and a couple of sacks in case of a blockage. If the car in front gets stuck you are stuck as well, so be prepared to leap out and lend a hand.

Some countries will not allow cars into the winter hills unless they are equipped with chains, and chains are expensive, so arrange to borrow or hire them at home, or be very sure they can be hired in the foothills, and that the hiring garages will be open at the time when you pass through. Leaving your car in the open in winter can cause trouble when you return, so try and find covered shelter. Switch off all the lights and electrics, and carry a set of jump leads to start the engine from another car, if the cold causes a flat battery. Spray door-locks with anti-freeze and then tape them over, to stop the latch freezing shut. The car should be well serviced and the battery charged before you set off. Attention to points like this gets the trip off to a good start, and ensures a pleasant finish, for nothing is more depressing when you are tired and eager to get home than to find that the car won't start. Leave some dry clothes and food in the car-boot for your return.

The trip plan

In the beginning was the objective. Money is less of a factor than time, and in the short winter days time is scarce and therefore valuable. Any plan must be fitted into the days away and the limited hours of daylight. If it doesn't fit, it can't be done and must be discarded for another. Since the travellers' choice lies between foot and skis, an outline plan for a one-week trip might look like this:

DAY			DISTANCE	
			Foot	*Ski*
SATURDAY	1	Arrive at base; get organised.	Nil	Nil
SUNDAY	2	Start late; short day.	16km. (10mi.)	16km. (10mi.)
MONDAY	3	Long day.	24km. (15mi.)	24km. (15mi.)
TUESDAY	4	Long day.	19km. (12mi.)	32km. (20mi.)
WEDNESDAY	5	Tired!!	16km. (10mi.)	24km. (15mi.)
THURSDAY	6	Pushing on.	19km. (12mi.)	32km. (20mi.)
FRIDAY	7	End in sight	19km. (12mi.)	32km. (20mi.)
SATURDAY	8	Early finish. Return to base.	8km. (5mi.)	16km. (10mi.)
SUNDAY	9	Go home.	Nil	Nil
		Total distance:	121km. (76mi.)	176km. (110mi.)

I put this up only as a discussion document but you must do the same, after considering the terrain and the weather and throwing in a good handful of that essential item, common sense. Use your own experience to tell you what you will be able to do in practice, and forget what you would like to do in theory. Winter is no place for overdoing it, but how much you can do is a personal thing, balanced against the needs of the group.

As a rough guide, I aim to travel no further in winter on skis than I would on foot in summer, the terrain being similar, while on foot I reduce my distances by anything from one-third to one-half, to take account of less daylight and unstable terrain.

Naismith's Rule

Naismith's Rule, as originally stated, said 'Allow one hour for every three miles measured off the map, plus half an hour for every 1000 ft of ascent'. This can be metricated into 5 km. per hour plus half an hour for every 300 metres. It should be remembered that this is an *unladen* estimate. To be applied exactly, the rule requires that the traveller counts contour lines; and the contour intervals, let it be

remembered, can vary from country to country. I have found
Naismith's Rule a useful basis in winter, but it must be adjusted to
allow for poor visibility and snow cover, both of which can slow the
traveller down.

I have discussed this point with a number of colleagues, and with
the usual reservations about fitness, skill, weather, terrain and so
on, all agree that Naismith's is, by and large, a good working rule.

The hard thing with all 'good working rules' is to obey them.
Experience tells us straight off the map that 16 km. (10 mi.) over
that terrain will be good going, yet we blithely commit ourselves to
24 km. (15 mi.) or 32 km. (20 mi.) on the second day, although we
must know that we will have slept badly, that the morning start will
be slow, that the wet tent will weigh a lot, and that on the second
day our unfitness hurts. Controlling these errors, and following
good working rules, is the leader's responsibility.

ROUTE CARD

Map sheet 125.		Start; Bog, Bala Farm.		Finish; Junction 894625
Start	Bearing	Finish	Distance	Time
896678	218°	Penny Hill 885659	2ks	1hr
885659	148°	Church 905652	3ks	1½hr
905652	308°	Post 875640	3ks	1½hr
875640	143°	Jnct 894625	4ks	2hr
Mag. Var. 7°W		Total time and distance	12ks	6hrs.

Route cards
Route cards, on a daily basis, should be prepared for the entire trip,
and checked. It is much easier to do this at home, on a table, than
out on some windswept hill or in a billowing tent. On the ground the
routes may have to be changed, but the basic route card is an
essential tool, and time taken to work it out and get the bearings
right is never wasted.

Escape routes and timings

No route card is complete in winter, or indeed at any time, without the inclusion of escape routes, listing refuges and safe ways down off tricky places. Time and distance forecasts must be checked out on the ground as each day wears on, for they are only estimates and must be amended if the facts prove them wrong.

On longer trips, over ten days or so, the group will get fitter, and can start to achieve longer daily distance targets and even gain ground. Over a weekend or on a one-week trip, it is more probable that the group will tire steadily, and this fact must be reflected on the route cards.

On the trail

The party should be awake before dawn, and ready to move as soon after first light as possible. Have a good breakfast, drink plenty of water and prepare the midday meal. Don't move before first light, as you may get lost or leave vital equipment behind, but use all the daylight there is to gain distance. Early in the day, before the sun can work on it, snow tends to be firm and crisp and easier to travel on. Move slowly but steadily, at a pace which the group can maintain, without overtiring or too much perspiration. Take it in turns to navigate, and to break trail, and check bearings if the mist starts to close in.

After half an hour the leader must call a short halt for the party to adjust gear, remove excess clothing or take a snack. Thereafter, apart from short pauses to admire the view, the group continues as a group until the midday halt. The fit should resist the temptation to forge far ahead, and the leader should gently urge on those who would lag behind. If everyone has enough breath to chat, and no one is getting overheated, the pace is about right.

The lunchtime halt should be fairly short, but everyone should remove their packs, put on windproofs, drink plenty of water and sit in the sunshine or, as the case may be, take shelter in some lee out of the wind.

During the day the snow state will certainly change, which may mean a waxing stop. Selecting the route carefully to stay on the hard snow can delay this moment in some circumstances. From early afternoon onwards, start looking for camp-sites. It is often possible

to spot a likely area from the map, but the actual site must be
selected on the ground. It is better to stop a little early, when you
find somewhere suitable, than forge on into the dusk in search of
something better.

Rest days
If you are on a hut-to-hut tour a rest day may not be necessary, for
the odd late start or early finish is usually sufficient. On a tent or
snow-hole trip it is usually necessary to fit in a rest day, if only to dry
out clothing or replenish stores. Allow one day a week for this,
aiming to descend on some village or hut just after noon, and not
leave again before well into the following morning. Running repairs
to equipment can also be carried out at this time, and it is a good
time to eat fresh food and have a party.

Navigation
Winter navigation is never easy. Visibility is often poor and the
leafless countryside changes shape under snow, quite apart from the
difficulties imposed by bad weather. Good maps, skill with the
compass, and accurate route cards are the fundamental tools. Move
slowly, checking off each landmark as it is positively identified and
aim to KNOW ALWAYS WHERE YOU ARE. The minute you feel
yourself to be lost, stop and replot your position, taking bearings to
establish your position before moving on.

To save time on the trail it is better to aim for one clear positive
landmark that you cannot miss, than attempt pin-point navigation
to some specific spot which, with winter visibility, is all too easily
missed. Daylight hours are precious.

Aim off to the right or left of your final objective, so that after,
for example, you arrive at the river bank, or line of hills which was
your general objective, you know which way to turn to find the hut
or refuge which is your specific objective, although the inevitable
circling tracks will usually point out in the right direction.

Winter walkers in the Spanish Pyrénées

And finally

This is a book about winter. Winter is not just a place for the downhill skier, the ice-climber and the ski-wanderer. Anyone can go out there and have a good time, given the equipment and techniques discussed in this book, and in so doing gradually acquire the experience necessary to live comfortably out of doors in all weathers. Technology has moved into the outdoor world, and the rough old days are probably gone for ever, but winter still retains an edge and drives her devotees back on to their own resources, physical and personal. Things *will* go wrong.

So, when the wind is up, the snow is driving and night is coming on, when you are fed up and far from home, remember that you're supposed to be enjoying yourself. I'll leave you with a quote from Chesterton:

'An adventure is an inconvenience considered differently'.

Have fun!

The Outdoor Companion, Rob Hunter (Constable 1979)

Ski Touring, William E. Osgood and L.J. Hurley (Tuttle, U.S.A., 1974)

Spur Book of Skiing, Rob Hunter and T. Brown (Spurbooks, 1976)

All About Winter Safety (Nordic Series, World Publications, U.S.A., 1975)

Joy of Backpacking, Dennis Look (Jalmar Press, U.S.A., 1976)

Ski Touring, Rob Hunter (Spurbooks, 1979)

How to Survive, Brian Hildreth (Puffin Books, 1976)

Cross Country Skiing, David Rees (Copp Clarke, Canada, 1975)

Don't Die on the Mountain (New Hampshire Chapter Appalachian Mountain Club, U.S.A., 1972)

A.B.C. of Avalanche Safety, E.R. La Chapelle (Colorado Sports, U.S.A., 1970)

Safety on the Hills (The Boy Scout Association, 1972)

Modern Snow and Ice Techniques, Bill March (Cicerone Press, 1973)

Spur Book of Weather Lore, Rob Hunter and T. Brown (Spurbooks, 1976)

The Weather Guide, A.G. Forsdyke (Hamlyn, 1969)

Wintering, Russ Mohney (Stackpole Books, U.S.A., 1976)

Safety on Mountains, John Jack et al, (British Mountaineering Council, 1974)

Mountaineering, Alan Blackshaw (Penguin, 1975)

Hiking the Teton Backcountry, Paul Lawrence (Sierra Club, U.S.A., 1973)

The Climate of Canada (Meteorological Branch, Toronto, Canada)

Avalanches and Snow Safety, Colin Fraser (John Murray, 1978)

Mountain Leadership, Eric Langmuir (Scottish Sports Council, 1976)

Safety in Outdoor Pursuits, Dept. of Education and Science (H.M.S.O., 1977)

Northern Survival (Dept. of Indian Affairs, Canada, 1972)

Ski the Norway (Norwegian Ski Council, Oslo, 1975)

Wilderness Skiing, Lito Tejada-Flores and Allan Steck (Sierra Club, U.S.A., 1972)

Map and Compass, Rob Hunter and T. Brown (Spurbooks, 1980)

The Whole Hiker's Handbook, William Kemsley Jr. (Morrow, U.S.A., 1979)

Snowshoeing, Gene Prater (The Mountaineers, Seattle, U.S.A., 1974)

Spur Book of Cross Country Skiing, Rob Hunter (Spurbooks, 1977)

Snowshoer's Equipment Guide (Sherpa Designs, 1975)

Cross Country Waxing and Maintenance, Wendy Williams (Contemporary Books, Chicago, U.S.A., 1977)

Avalanche Handbook The U.S. Dept. of Agriculture Forest Service.

Elementary Meteorology, Her Majesty's Stationery Office, H.M.S.O. London.

Wilderness Tips (The Adirondack Mountain Club, Glenn Falls, N.Y., U.S.A.)

Mountain and Cave Rescue (Mountain Rescue Committee, U.K., 1975)

Hypothermia, Theodore C. Lathrop, M.D. (Mazamas, U.S.A., 1975)

Cross Country Skiing, Ned Gillette (Draden, U.K., 1980)

Frostbite, Bradford Washburn (Museum of Science, Boston, U.S.A., 1963)

Winter Hiking and Camping, John Danielsen (Adirondack Mountain Club, U.S.A., 1977)

Snow Camping, Cameron McNeish (Spurbooks, 1980)

Complete Snow Camping Guide, Ray Bridge (Scribners, U.S.A., 1973)

Cross-County Skiing Today, John Caldwell (The Stephen Greene Press, Brattleboro, Vermont, 1977)

Be Expert with Map and Compass, Bjorn Kjellstrom (Scribners, U.S.A., 1975)

The Wilderness Route Finder, Calvin Rutstrum (Collier MacMillan, U.K., 1977)

We Learned to Ski, H. Evans, B. Jackman and M. Ottaway (Collins, U.K. 1975)

Adventure Travel, Pat Dickerman (Thomas Crowell, U.S.A., 1978)

Walking, Hiking and Backpacking, Anthony Greenbank
 (Constable, 1977)
Modern First Aid, A.S. Playfair (Hamlyn, 1975)

For keeping up to date with developments in equipment and technique, for articles on trips and details of current prices and stockists, a subscription to a good outdoor magazine is advisable.

U.K.
Climber and Rambler, 12 York St, Glasgow G2 8LG

The Great Outdoors, 12 York St, Glasgow G2 8LG

Camping, Link House, Dingwall Avenue, Croydon, Surrey CR9 2TA

Practical Camper, 38/42 Hampton Road, Teddington, Middx. TW11 0FE

Ski Magazine, Ocean Publications, 34 Buckingham Palace Road, London SW1

Ski Survey, The Ski Club of Great Britain, 118 Eaton Sq., London SW1N 0RE

U.S.A.
Backpacker Magazine, 65 Adam St, Bedford Hills, New York 10507, U.S.A.

Adventure Travel, 444 N.E. Ravenna Blvd, Seattle, Washington 98115, U.S.A.

Ski Magazine, P.O. Box 2795, Boulder, Colorado 80302, U.S.A.

Summit Magazine, P.O. Box 1889, Big Bear Lake, California 92315, U.S.A.

XC Skier, 370 7th Ave., New York, N.Y. 10001, U.S.A.

Canada
Outdoor Canada, 953A Eglington Ave. East, Toronto, Ontario, Canada N4P 1J9

The Country Code

1. Guard against all risks of fire.
2. Fasten all gates.
3. Keep dogs under proper control.
4. Keep to paths across farmland.
5. Avoid damaging fences, hedges and walls.
6. Leave no litter.
7. Protect wildlife, wide plants and trees.
8. Go carefully on country roads.
9. Respect the life of the countryside.
10. Safeguard all water supplies; never pollute or foul lakes, streams, rivers or reservoirs.

The Mountain Code

1. Do not undertake anything which is beyond your training and experience.
2. Ensure that your equipment is sound.
3. Know the rescue facilities available in the area you are in and the procedures in case of accidents.
4. Know first-aid.
5. Never go into the mountains alone.
6. Leave details of your route and proposed time of return with a responsible person. Do not forget to report your safe return.
7. Be competent in the use of map and compass and rely on your compass.
8. Lead only those climbs and walks which you are competent to lead.
9. Ensure that loud voices and radios do not disturb the quiet of the countryside.
10. Do not throw stones and dislodge boulders.
11. Do not pollute water.
12. Do not interfere with others when climbing – wait your turn.
13. Know the local weather forecast and do not hesitate to turn back or abandon the trip.
14. Know the conditions on the mountain and master the use of ice axe, crampons and rope-work.
15. Camp on official sites or obtain permission from the owner.
16. Be considerate in the siting of latrines and replace the turf.
17. Be aware of the dangers of fire.
18. Do not remove the wild plants, flowers or trees or damage them.
20. Avoid startling farm livestock and disturbing wildlife.

Appendix 1

Kit Lists

These lists are for selected purposes only. It is *not* suggested that the traveller carries all these items all the time.

Possible group stores are marked with the letter 'g'. For the winter features of individual items you must refer to the relevant chapters.

Clothing

Boots
Laces
Stockings (3 pairs)
Insoles (2 pairs)
Underwear (2 sets)
Breeches *or*
  Trousers *or*
  Salopettes
Duvet (down or synthetic) *or*
  Fibre-pile jacket *or*
  Anorak
Belt
Braces
Shirts
Sweater
Repair outfit (g)

Cagoule
Overtrousers
Wind shirt
Gaiters
Face mask
Spare clothing
Stuff sacks
Overboots
Hat *or*
Balaclava
Scarf
Gloves (2 pairs)
Inner gloves
Goggles
Glasses
Handerkerchiefs

Camping

Rucksack with liner
Tent (g)
Pegs (g)
Poles (g)
Sleeping bag (down or synthetic)
Mattress
Stove (g)
Fuel bottle

Torch
Batteries and bulbs (g)
Candles
Lighters
Matches
Plastic bags (g)
Washing and shaving gear
Vacuum flask

Cookset (g)
Eating equipment
Funnel (g)
Food (g)
Cleaning gear (g)

Toilet paper
Tissues
Double guying line (g)
Water purification tablets (g)
Water bottles

Travel and navigation

Maps (g)
Map case (g)
Compass
Notebook
Pencil

Route cards (g)
Passports
Club membership cards
Tickets
Money
Insurance documents

Hardware and Skis

Crampons, 10-point
Snow shovel (g)
Poles
Skins
Snow shoes
Snow-saw (g)

Ice axe
Skis, cross-country or alpine
Waxes (g)
Spare ski-tip (g)
Spare cable (g)
Spare binding wishbone (g)
Epoxy resin or glue (g)

Safety and survival

First-aid kit (g)
Survival kit (Ten Essentials)
Barometer (g)
Radio (g)

Bivvy bag
Space blankets (g)
Avalanche cords
Avalanche Sondes (s)
Probes
45 metres of 11 mm. Kernmantel
rope (g)

Sundries

Camera (g)
Film (g)
Paperbacks (g)
Hip flask

Field glasses (g)
Razor
Salt tablets (g)
Sun cream (g)
Repair kit (g)

Appendix 2

Winter training facilities

U.K.

Ancrum Outdoor Education Centre, 10 Ancrum Rd, Dundee, Tayside, Scotland. (Canoeing, mountaineering, skiing, environmental studies.)

Field Studies Council, Montford Bridge, Shrewsbury. (Ten residential centres instructing in wildlife, botany, geology, mountain walking, marine biology, photography, exploring.)

Mountain Rescue Committee, 9 Milldale Ave., Temple Meads, Buxton, Derbyshire.

Glenmore Lodge Scottish National Outdoor Training Centre, Aviemore, Inverness-shire PH2 1QU, Scotland. (Courses on skiing, ski-mountaineering, hill walking, snow and ice climbing, mountain rescue, rock climbing.)

Whitehall Outdoor Centre, Longhill, Buxton, Derbyshire. (Caving, climbing, and all outdoor pursuits.)

Peak District National Park Study Centre, Loosehill Hall, Castleton, Derbyshire. (Courses on outdoor activities and pursuits.)

Outward Bound Mountain School, Holmbrook, Eskdale, Cumbria.

Outward Bound Mountain School, Ullswater, nr. Penrith, Cumbria.

The Christian Mountain Centre, Tremadog, Porthmadog, Gwynedd, North Wales. (Environmental studies and outdoor education.)

Yorkshire Dales National Park, Whernside Manor, Dent, Sedbergh, Cumbria. (Caving and potholing.)

Plas Y Brenin National Centre for Mountain Activities, Capel Curig, Betws-y-Coed, Gwynedd. (Various courses for all mountain users.)

Outdoor Pursuits Centre, Eridge Green, Tunbridge Wells, Kent TN3 9LW. (Climbing courses on sandstone outcrops close to London.)

National Caving Association, Dept. of Geography, University of Birmingham, Box No. 363, Birmingham 15.

Mountainwalking Leader Training Board, (MLTB) Crawford House, Precinct Centre, Manchester University, Booth St East, Manchester M13 9RZ.

Scottish Mountain Leader Training Board, 1 St Colme St, Edinburgh EH3 6AA.

Northern Ireland Mountain Leader Training Board, 49 Malone Road, Belfast BT9 6RZ.

U.S.A. and Canada

Museum of Northern Arizona Expeditions, Dept. BP Rt. 4, Box 720, Flagstaff, Arizona 86001, U.S.A. (Backpacking, ski touring, rafting, natural history.)

Rocky Mountain Backpack Tours, P.O. Box 2781, Evergreen, Colorado 80439, U.S.A. (Backpacking expeditions along the Great Divide.)

Big Bend Rio Grande Raft Trips, 2220 Birch, Denver, Colorado 80207, U.S.A. (Ski touring and winter mountaineering.)

Iowa Mountaineers, P.O. Box 163, Iowa City, Iowa, U.S.A. (Mountaineering, hiking and venture travel.)

National Outdoor Leadership School, Box AA, Dept. B., Lander, Wyoming, U.S.A. (Wilderness expeditions.)

Outdoor Experience, 62 RT. 22, Greenbrook, New Jersey, U.S.A. (Rock climbing, ice climbing, backpacking.)

Expeditions Canada, 51 Overton Crescent, Don Mills, Ontario, Canada. (Backpacking.)

Marin Adventure, College of Marin, Kentfield, California, U.S.A. (Nature, backpacking, environmental studies.)

Outdoor Program, Calgary University, Calgary, Alberta, Canada.

Appendix 3

Clubs and tour operators
These clubs and tour operating companies can offer good advice to
winter travellers, or organise trips to suitable countries abroad.
They, or their brochures and magazines, are also good sources of
information for winter trips.

U.K.

The Austrian Alpine Club (U.K. Section), 13 Longcroft House,
　　Fretherne Road, Welwyn Garden City, Herts. AL8 6PQ.
Norwegian State Railways Travel Bureau (U.K. Office), 21/24
　　Cockspur St, London SW1.
British Mountaineering Club, Crawford House, Precinct Centre,
　　Booth St East, Manchester 13.
Backpackers' Club, 20 St Michael's Road, Tilehurst, Reading,
　　Berks. RG3 4RP.
Ramblers Association, 1/5 Wandsworth Road, London SW8 2LJ.
Ramblers Holidays, 13 Longcroft House, Fretherne Road, Welwyn
　　Garden City, Herts. AL8 6PQ.
Waymark Holidays Ltd, 295 Lillie Road, London SW6.
Youth Hostels Association, 8 St Stephen's Hill, St Albans, Herts.
Ski Club of Great Britain, 118 Eaton Square, London SW1 W9AF.
Scottish Highlands and Islands Development Board, Bridge House,
　　27 Bank St, Inverness 1VI 1QR, Scotland.
Highland Guides, Aviemore, Inverness, Scotland.

Finland

Finn-Ski, c/o Twickenham Travel Ltd, 84 Hampton Road,
　　Twickenham, Middx. TW2 5QS.

France

Federation Française de la Randonnée Pédestre (CNSGR), 92 Rue
de Clignancourt, 75883 Paris 18, France.
Club Alpin Français, 7 Rue la Bóetie, Paris 775008, France.
Touring Club de France, 65 Avenue de la Grande Armée, 75782
Paris, France.

Germany

Verband Deutscher Wandervereine, Hospital Strasse 21B, 7000
Stuttgart 1, Germany.

Iceland

Utivist (Outdoor Tours), 6 Laekjargata, Reykjavik, Iceland.

Italy

Federazione Italiana Escursionismo, 10143 Via Cibrario 33, Turin,
Italy.

Norway

Norwegian State Railways Travel Bureau, 21/24 Cockspur St,
London SW1.
Den Norske Turistföreningen (DNT), Stortingsgate 28, Oslo 1,
Norway.

Spain

Federacion Española de Montanismo, Alberto Aguilera 3, Madrid
15, Spain.

Sweden

Svenska Turistföreningen, Fack, S-10380 Stockholm, Sweden.

Switzerland

Schweizerische Arbeitsgemeinschaft Wanderswege (SAW), Im
    Hirshalm 49, 4125 Riehan, Switzerland.

U.S.A.

The American Hiking Society, 1701 18th St, N.W., Washington
    D.C. 20009, U.S.A.
National Hiking and Ski Touring Association, P.O. Box 7421,
    Colorado Springs, Colorado 80907, U.S.A.
Appalachian Trails Conference, P.O. Box 236, Harpers Ferry,
    W.Va.25425, U.S.A.
Adirondack Mountain Club, 1 Ridge Road, Glenn Falls, New York
    12801, U.S.A.

National tourist boards
These countries all have good terrain and climatic conditions,
suitable for winter trips.

Austrian National Tourist Office
30 St George Street
London W1R 9FA

Canadian Office of Tourism
Canada House
Trafalgar Square London SW1

Czechoslovak Travel Bureau
17–18 Bond St
London W1

Finnish Tourist Board
53 54 Haymarket
London SW1Y 4RP

French Government Tourist Office
178 Piccadilly
London W1V 0AL

German National Tourist Office
61 Conduit St
London W1R 0EN

Iceland Tourist Information Bureau
73 Grosvenor St
London W1X 9DD

Italian State Tourist Office
201 Regent St
London W1

Norwegian National Tourist Office
20 Pall Mall
London SW1Y 5NE

Spanish National Tourist Office
57–58 St James St
London SW1A 1LD

Swiss National Tourist Office
Swiss Centre
1 New Coventry St
London W1V 3HG

United States Tourist Service
22 Sackville St
London W1

Yugoslav National Tourist Office
143 Regent St
London W1

Winter Equipment Stockists listed by town

Key (H) = EQUIPMENT FOR HIRE.

ABERDEEN

Bill Marshall,
306 George Street, (H)

Rad Sports,
30 Market Street,

ALTRINCHAM

Nick Estcourt Outdoor Sports,
84 Stamford New Road.

AMBLESIDE

The Climbers Shop,
Compston Corner. (H)

ASHTON-UNDER-LYNE

Millins Outdoor Pursuits,
Langham Street.
(next to ASDA)

BEDFORD

Jeans (of Bedford)
40 Allhallows.

BIRMINGHAM

Eiger Sport,
47 Stephenson Street.

Ellis Brigham
18–19 Snow Hill,
Queensway.

Pindisports,
27–29 Martineau Square.

Y.H.A.
35 Cannon Street. (H)

BLACKPOOL

The Alpine Centre,
193/5 Church Street.

BRADFORD

Allan Austin,
Jacob St. Mills,
Manchester Road.

BRIGHTON

Alpine Sports,
138 Western Road, (H)

Eurosport (Backpacking) Ltd.,
66/67 North Road.

BRISTOL

Ellis Brigham,
162 Whiteladies Road,
Blackboy Hill. (H)

Pindisports,
5 Welsh Back.

Tratman & Lowther,
Berkeley Place.

BURNLEY

Sportak,
25 Hammerton Street.

BUXTON

Jo Royle,
High Peak Outdoor Centre,
22 High Street.

CAMBRIDGE

Pindisports,
Mitchams Corner,
34 Chesterton Road.

Cambridge Outdoor Centre,
7 Bridge Street.

CAPEL CURIG

Joe Brown,
Capel Curig,
N. Wales.

CARDIFF

Youth Hostels Ass.
South Wales Region,
131 Woodville Road,

Cardiff Sportsgear,
81 Whitechurch Road.

CHESTER

Ellis Brigham
7 Northgate Row.

COVENTRY

Mountain Sports,
61 Empress Buildings,
Binley Road.

CROYDON

Pindisports,
1098 Whitgift Centre.

DERBY

Alpine Action,
201 Normanton Road,
DE3 6US.

Derby Mountain Centre,
85 King Street.

Prestidge,
350 Normanton Road. (H)

DUNDEE

David Low Sports,
21 Commercial Street. (H)

EDINBURGH

Blues/Alpine Sports,
1 Wemyss Place,
West end of Queen Street.

Ian Luke Sports,
28 Howe Street. (H)

Graham Tiso,
13 Wellington Place,
Leith.

ELGIN

Andy Main,
11 Commerce Street.

EXETER

Grays of Exeter,
181–182 Sidwell Street.

FORT WILLIAM

Nevisport
72 High Street, PH33 6EA.

GERRARDS X

Woodward & Stalder,
4 Packhorse Road.

GLASGOW

Alpine Sports,
450 Sauchiehall Street.

Nevisport,
261 Sauchiehall Street.

Ian Luke Sports,
170 Battlefield Road. (H)

HALESOWEN

Casac Equipment
3 Hagley Road.

HALIFAX

The Outdoor Centre,
3 Princess Arcade.

HARROGATE

E.H. Adventure Sports,
71 Station Parade.

HEMEL HEMPSTED

Don Farrell Ltd,
254 Marlowes.

HIGH WYCOMBE

Woodward & Stalder,
Castle Street.

INVERNESS

Clive Rowland Outdoor Sports,
60 Academy Street.

JOHNSTONE

Boat Road Supplies,
Canal Road.

KENDAL

Waterside Adventure Sports,
Waterside.

KESWICK

Mountain World,
28 Lake Road.

LANCASTER

H. Robinson,
4/5 New Road,
LA1 1EZ.

LEEDS

Centresport,
Merrion Centre (H)
Woodhouse Lane.

LEICESTER

Roger Turner (Leics) Ltd.
52a London Road.

LIVERPOOL

Smith & Beyer,
43a Harrington Street 2.

Ellis Brigham
73 Bold Street,
City Centre. (H)

LONDON

Alpine Sports,
114 Brompton Road,
SW3 1JJ. (H)

Alpine Sports,
10/12 Holborn
EC1. (H)

Alpine Sports,
215 Kensington High Street,
W8. (H)

Pindisports,
14 Holborn,
EC1.

Pindisports,
373 5 Uxbridge Road,
Acton W3.

Y.H.A.
14 Southampton Street,
WC1. (H)

MANCHESTER

Ellis Brigham, 12/14 Cathedral Street.

Stubbs Outdoor Sports,
211 Deansgate.

Y.H.A.
Deansgate (H)

MATLOCK

Bivouac Outdoor Life,
77a Dale Road.

MIDDLESBOROUGH

Cleveland Mountain Sports,
98 Newport Road. (H)

NEWCASTLE-UPON-TYNE

LD Mountain Centre,
34 Dean Street,
NE1 1PG. (H)

NORTHAMPTON

White & Bishop,
13–17 Bridge Street.

NOTTINGHAM

Roger Turner Mountain Sports,
120 Derby Road
NG1 5FB.

OXFORD

Westsports
274 Banbury Road,
Summertown.

PAIGNTON

Harbour Sports Paignton,
The Harbour.

PENRITH

Lake Mountain Sports Ltd.,
Middlegate.

PERTH

Banks of Perth,
29 St. John Street.

Rad Sports,
21 George Street.

PONTEFRACT

M & T Crossley Tordoff,
Newgate.

PRESTON

Glacier Sport,
40/41 Lune Street.

Preston Camping Centre,
49 53 Corporation Street.

READING

Carters Camping & Ski-ing Centre,
99 Caversham Road. (H)

Pindisports, (at Hornes)
1 Oxford Road.

ROSSENDALE

Ellis Brigham
The Ski Lodge,
Haslingden Old Road,
Rawtenstall.

ST. ALBANS

Jeans (St. Albans) Ltd.,
14 Victoria Street.

SHEFFIELD

Thomas & Taylor,
24 Fitzwilliam Gate,
S1 4JH.

SKIPTON

The Dales Outdoor Centre,
Coach Street,
BD23 1LH.

STOCKPORT

Alpenstock,
2 Port Street.

Base Camp,
89 Lower Hillgate.

STOKE-ON-TRENT

Jo Royle,
25 Brunswick Street.

SUNDERLAND

Reynolds Outdoor Centre,
6 Derwent Street,
SR1 3NT (H)

SWINDON

Westsports,
17 Fleet Street.

YORK

Wilderness Ways,
9 Colliergate.

Index